Sams **Teach Yourself**

Facebook®

in **10 Minutes**

Third Edition

800 East 96th Street, Indianapolis, Indiana 46240

Sams Teach Yourself Facebook® in 10 Minutes, Third Edition

Copyright © 2012 by Pearson Education, Inc.

All rights reserved. No part of this book shall be reproduced, stored in a retrieval system, or transmitted by any means, electronic, mechanical, photocopying, recording, or otherwise, without written permission from the publisher. No patent liability is assumed with respect to the use of the information contained herein. Although every precaution has been taken in the preparation of this book, the publisher and author assume no responsibility for errors or omissions. Nor is any liability assumed for damages resulting from the use of the information contained herein.

ISBN-13: 978-0-672-33584-6
ISBN-10: 0-672-33584-0

Library of Congress Cataloging-in-Publication Data:

Gunter, Sherry Kinkoph.

  Sams teach yourself Facebook in 10 minutes / Sherry Kinkoph-Gunter. — 3rd ed.

      p. cm.—(Sams teach yourself)

  ISBN 978-0-672-33584-6—ISBN 0-672-33584-0 1. Facebook (Electronic resource) 2. Online social networks. 3. Social networks—Computer network resources. 4. Web sites—Design. I. Title. II. Title: Facebook in 10 minutes.

  HM742.G86 2012

  006.7'54—dc23

                                    2012007174

Printed in the United States of America

First Printing March 2012

Trademarks

All terms mentioned in this book that are known to be trademarks or service marks have been appropriately capitalized. Pearson Education, Inc. cannot attest to the accuracy of this information. Use of a term in this book should not be regarded as affecting the validity of any trademark or service mark.

Warning and Disclaimer

Every effort has been made to make this book as complete and as accurate as possible, but no warranty or fitness is implied. The information provided is on an "as is" basis. The author and the publisher shall have neither liability nor responsibility to any person or entity with respect to any loss or damages arising from the information contained in this book.

Bulk Sales

Pearson Education, Inc. offers excellent discounts on this book when ordered in quantity for bulk purchases or special sales. For more information, please contact

    U.S. Corporate and Government Sales
    1-800-382-3419
    corpsales@pearsontechgroup.com

For sales outside the United States, please contact

    International Sales
    international@pearsoned.com

Editor-in-Chief
Greg Wiegand

Acquisitions Editor
Michelle Newcomb

Development Editor
Robin Drake

Managing Editor
Sandra Schroeder

Senior Project Editor
Tonya Simpson

Copy Editor
Paula Lowell

Proofreader
Sarah Kearns

Indexer
Lisa Stumpf

Technical Editor
Vince Averello

Publishing Coordinator
Cindy Teeters

Book Designer
Gary Adair

Compositor
Mark Shirar

Contents

Introduction   **1**

1 **Introduction to Facebook**   **5**
   What Is Facebook? 5
   Facebook History 7
   Facebook Features 8
   Tour the Facebook Site 9

2 **Setting Up a Facebook Account**   **13**
   Signing Up for an Account 13
   Building Your Profile Page 19
   Accessing Your Account Info 26

3 **Finding Help with Facebook Services and Etiquette**   **29**
   Understanding Facebook's Terms of Service 29
   Facebook Etiquette 32
   Finding Help with the Help Center 34

4 **Navigating Your Timeline**   **39**
   Timeline Basics 39
   Working with Stories 47

5 **Navigating the Home Page**   **51**
   Understanding Facebook Information Flow 51
   Understanding the Home Page 52
   Working with Your News Feeds 58
   Viewing and Controlling Notifications 60

6 **Connecting with Friends**   **63**
   Finding Friends 63
   Viewing and Editing Friends 68

7 **Guarding Your Privacy**   **77**

Understanding Privacy and Security Settings
on Facebook 77

Customizing Your Privacy Settings 81

Reporting Abuse 90

8 **Communicating Through Facebook**   **91**

How to Communicate on Facebook 91

Sending and Receiving Messages 92

Sharing Links 96

Blogging with Notes 98

Chatting with Friends 101

9 **Sharing Photos**   **105**

Sharing Photos on Facebook 105

Viewing the Photos Page 108

Adding Your Own Photos 110

Using Other Photo Uploaders 113

Tagging Photos 114

Organizing and Editing Your Photos 116

10 **Sharing Videos**   **123**

Sharing Videos on Facebook 123

Adding a Video 124

Viewing Videos 127

Editing Your Videos 129

Recording a New Video 131

11 **Joining Groups**   **135**

Socializing with Facebook Groups 135

Finding a Group 138

Joining a Group 138

Starting Your Own Group 141

Managing Your Group 145

12 Tracking Events **151**

Events Overview 151

Finding Events 153

Creating Your Own Events 156

Managing Your Events 159

13 Adding Applications **161**

What Are Apps? 161

Kinds of Apps 162

Finding Apps 164

Managing Apps 169

14 Understanding Pages **173**

Page Basics 173

Finding and Following Pages 177

Creating and Managing a Page 179

15 The Facebook Marketplace **189**

What Is the Marketplace? 189

Navigating the Marketplace 191

Browsing the Listings 193

Adding Your Own Listing 195

16 Making Facebook Mobile **197**

Overview of Facebook's Mobile Features 197

Activating Facebook Mobile for Text Messages 199

Sending Text Messages from a Mobile Device 202

Uploading Photos or Videos 203

Index **205**

About the Author

Sherry Kinkoph Gunter has written and edited oodles of books over the past 20 years covering a wide variety of computer topics, including Microsoft Office programs, digital photography, and web applications. Her recent titles include *Easy Microsoft Word 2010, Craigslist 4 Everyone, Teach Yourself VISUALLY Microsoft Office 2007*, and *Microsoft Office 2008 for Mac Bible*. Sherry began writing computer books back in 1992 for Macmillan, and her flexible writing style has allowed her to author for a varied assortment of imprints and formats. Sherry's ongoing quest is to aid users of all levels in the mastering of ever-changing computer technologies, helping users make sense of it all and get the most out of their machines and online experiences. Sherry currently resides in a swamp in the wilds of east central Indiana with a lovable ogre and a menagerie of interesting creatures. Sherry is also hopelessly addicted to Facebook.

Dedication

Special thanks go out to Michelle Newcomb, for allowing me the opportunity to tackle this third edition of a very fun project; development editor Robin Drake, for her dedication and patience in shepherding this project; to copy editor Paula Lowell, for ensuring that all the i's were dotted and t's were crossed; to technical editor Vince Averello, for skillfully checking each step and offering valuable input along the way; and finally to the production team at Pearson, for their talents in creating such a helpful, much-needed, and incredibly good-looking book. Also, special thanks to all my Facebook friends (you know who you are) and their avid interest in helping with this project. Finally, extra-special thanks to my loveable cohort, Shrek (a.k.a. Matty), for his constant support and irrepressible humor.

We Want to Hear from You!

As the reader of this book, *you* are our most important critic and commentator. We value your opinion and want to know what we're doing right, what we could do better, what areas you'd like to see us publish in, and any other words of wisdom you're willing to pass our way.

You can email or write me directly to let me know what you did or didn't like about this book—as well as what we can do to make our books stronger.

Please note that I cannot help you with technical problems related to the topic of this book, and that due to the high volume of mail I receive, I might not be able to reply to every message.

When you write, please be sure to include this book's title and author as well as your name and phone or email address. I will carefully review your comments and share them with the author and editors who worked on the book.

Email: consumer@samspublishing.com

Mail: Greg Wiegand
          Editor-in-Chief
          Sams Publishing
          800 East 96th Street
          Indianapolis, IN 46240 USA

Reader Services

Visit our website and register this book at informit.com/register for conve-
nient access to any updates, downloads, or errata that might be available
for this book.

Introduction

With more than 800 million active users and growing, ignoring the buzz about Facebook (www.facebook.com) is hard. It's an ever-present topic these days, and it shows no signs of letting up. If you're ready to get to the bottom of this Internet sensation and find out how to use this social networking phenomenon for yourself, this is the book for you. Social networks are a bit daunting at first, but don't worry. This book shows you how to navigate the site and make use of its various features in no time at all. By the end, you'll feel as if you can Facebook with the best of them!

About This Book

As part of the *Sams Teach Yourself in 10 Minutes* guides, this book aims to teach you the ins and outs of using Facebook without wasting a lot of precious time. Divided into easy-to-handle lessons that you can tackle in 10 minutes each, you learn the following Facebook tasks and topics:

▶ How to painlessly set up a Facebook account

▶ How to create and manage a profile page, including how to add a profile picture and work with the new timeline

▶ How to connect with friends and make new ones, plus organize them into specialized lists

▶ How to communicate by messaging, chatting, and posting status updates

▶ How to track what your friends are doing and what they're up to on Facebook

▶ How to upload photos, links, and videos to share with friends

▶ How to share your common interests and hobbies through groups

▶ How to add applications to get more out of your Facebook experience

► How to sell and buy stuff in the Marketplace

► How to use Facebook's mobile features

► How to create pages for a professional business or organization

► How to keep yourself safe and protect your privacy on Facebook

► How to conduct yourself on the site and follow Facebook's terms of service and unspoken etiquette rules

After completing these lessons, you'll know everything you need to know to get the most out of your time on Facebook.

Who This Book Is For

This book is geared toward anyone interested in learning his or her way around Facebook. Whether you're a new user or a seasoned participant, or you're just learning how to navigate the new and improved interface, this book shows you each major feature of the site and how to make use of it. For example, have you always wanted to start your own group? Have you ever wondered how to invite people to a party? Or have you always wanted to look for more applications to try but didn't know how to find them? You'll learn how to do these tasks and more.

Each lesson focuses on a particular subject, such as communicating on Facebook or using the Photos application. You can skip around from topic to topic, or read the book from start to finish.

How to Use This Book

To use this book, all you really need is a healthy dose of curiosity to find out what you can do on Facebook. To use Facebook itself, you'll need a computer (PC or Mac), a web browser (any kind will do), and an Internet connection. That's it. Facebook is free to use, so if you have those three things, you're all set and ready to go.

If you use a smartphone, iPhone, or iPad, you can also tap into Facebook's features.

Conventions Used in This Book

Whenever you need to click a particular button or link in Facebook, you'll find the label or name for that item bolded in the text, such as "click the **Delete** button." In addition to the text and figures in this book, you'll also encounter some special boxes labeled Tip, Note, or Caution.

> TIP: Tips offer helpful shortcuts or easier ways to do something.

> NOTE: Notes are extra bits of information related to the text that might help you expand your knowledge or understanding.

> CAUTION: Cautions are warnings or other important information you need to know about consequences of using a feature or executing a task.

Screen Captures

The figures captured for this book are mainly from the Internet Explorer web browser (version 9.0) or from the Safari web browser (version 5.0.5). If you use a different browser, your screens might look slightly different.

Also keep in mind that the developers of Facebook are constantly working to improve the website. New features are added regularly, and old ones change or disappear. This means the pages change often, including the elements found on each, so your own screens may differ from the ones shown in this book. Don't be too alarmed, however. The basics, though they are tweaked in appearance from time to time, stay mostly the same in principle and use.

LESSON 1

Introduction to Facebook

In this lesson, you learn about the Facebook phenomenon, where Facebook came from, and what you can do with it.

What Is Facebook?

Facebook (www.facebook.com) is a social networking website. To flesh out this definition a bit more, it's an online community—a place where people can meet and interact; swap photos, videos, and other information; and generally connect with friends, family, coworkers, fellow students, fellow hobbyists and enthusiasts, and numerous others in their social network. Facebook connects people within cities or regions, work or school, home or abroad, and so on. Built on an architecture of profile pages that allow individual users to share information about themselves and communicate with others, Facebook seeks to create an environment in which members log in regularly to keep track of what friends and colleagues are doing, share their own activities, interact about interests and hobbies, send messages, and join groups and networks—just to name a few things.

Facebook is the number-one social networking site on the Internet. Offering free access and dozens of tools for connecting people in social, school, and workplace environments, Facebook has more than 800 million active users and is growing, with 500 million logging in daily to use the site. More than 250 million users access Facebook through mobile devices. Perhaps you're wondering at this point why so many people are flocking to Facebook. That's easy: It's simple to use, a fun way to connect with others, and incredibly powerful.

What started out as a college-based social networking site, most of Facebook's members are now outside the college startup base and include users of all ages and walks of life. More than half of Facebook users are over the age of 25.

More than 70 translations of the site are up and running, making it a global phenomenon. Currently, 75% of users are outside the United States, but those numbers are changing as Facebook continues to rapidly catch on stateside.

At its heart, Facebook is all about connecting people with people. Facebook users do a variety of things with the site: track news about friends far and wide; make new friends, often based on common interests; share photos, music, links, and videos; organize and invite people to events; play games; spread the word about charities and causes; buy and sell stuff; market products; and much, much more. According to Facebook's own statistics, more than 30 billion pieces of content are shared each day, including photos, links, news stories, blog posts, and such. The average user generates about 90 pieces of content per month and interacts with 80 community pages, groups, and events.

The business community is also jumping into the Facebook frenzy, utilizing the site as a tool to connect to customers and clientele. Sixty percent of the world's top retailers post Facebook content, and a growing number of companies are advertising on the site, increasing exposure and enhancing their brands and business relationships. If you're a business owner, you can create profile pages specific to your business to interact with customers, get feedback, and make your presence known. In Facebook terminology, these specialized profiles are called Pages.

As a website, Facebook is accessible to all Internet users, where permitted. In addition to connecting people, third-party developers are creating a wide variety of applications—programs that run within the Facebook framework—to entertain and inform. Applications range from the silly to the serious, and new ones are added each day. Facebook users install more than 20 million applications on any given day. 190 countries build on the Facebook platform, and more than 2.5 million websites have integrated with the social networking site, with 10,000 more added each day.

Those are astounding growth statistics, right? Add to that fact an award-winning movie (*The Social Network*, 2010), and you get a seriously popular website, second only to Google in overall traffic. What makes Facebook such a huge hit are its features and tools and the eagerness of its users to network with each other in their communities locally and globally.

Facebook History

Social networks have been around for a while now, and most are focused on connecting friends and colleagues. In prehistoric times (the '80s and '90s), Bulletin Board Services (BBS) and Usenet groups were examples of early forms of social networks. As the concept evolved, generalized communities, such as Geocities and Tripod (back in the mid-1990s), brought people together through chat rooms and forums. Today, social networks are flourishing all over the Web, including the ever-popular Twitter, LinkedIn, MySpace, and Google+. Some social sites, such as Classmates.com, specialize in connecting former schoolmates, whereas other social sites, such as SixDegrees.com, focus on indirect ties between people. Some sites specialize in niche groups, whereas others aim for more generalized populations of people. Internet business strategies are recognizing the opportunities inherent in social networks and are happy to cater to different groups of people and their networking needs.

So where does Facebook fit in? Facebook is the front runner in the social networking race. Originally called "The Facebook," Facebook started out in 2004 as a network geared toward college students at Harvard University. Founded by a computer science major, Mark Zuckerberg, and his roommates, Dustin Moskovitz and Chris Hughes, the project quickly gained popularity among students. With financing assistance from Eduardo Saverin, the site grew seemingly overnight.

The original idea was based on hardcopy "*face books*" commonly used to acquaint students with the campus community, including staff, faculty, and incoming students. Initially, the website was available only to Harvard students, but rapidly expanded to other universities in the Boston, Massachusetts, area. Eventually, the concept spread to other universities and high schools, and today, anyone with a valid email address can join the fray. Facebook swiftly became an Internet sensation, and in 2005, the facebook.com domain was purchased and the base of operations moved to California.

Although the site is free to join, it generates revenue through advertising, including banner ads. New features and updates are added regularly, and the Facebook folks are quick to heed the ideas, wants, and needs of its members. In 2007, the Facebook Platform was launched, providing a framework for software developers to create applications for the site. Today, tens of thousands of applications are available for Facebook, with more added daily. Rolling out a rework of its profile pages into a timeline-skewed design at the end of 2011, Facebook continues to evolve and generate excitement.

Facebook Features

So what does a Facebook member do on the site? What exactly does the site have to offer? More importantly, what can you get out of the experience? Here's a list of various activities and pursuits to get you started on the road to answers to those questions:

- ▶ Connect with people. Connect with friends, family, colleagues, and fellow students. Reconnect with old friends, acquaintances, and family members scattered about the globe. Make new friends who share your interests.

- ▶ Keep track of your friends' activities, while they keep track of yours.

- ▶ Share messages, links, photo albums, and video clips.

- ▶ Blog with the Facebook Notes feature.

- ▶ Organize events and invite friends to parties, concerts, band performances, meetings, and gatherings of all kinds.

- ▶ Play games with friends.

- ▶ Send virtual gifts, birthday greetings, and other digital objects.

- ▶ Join in groups and networks to connect with people sharing similar interests.

- ▶ Become a fan of a celebrity, politician, band, television show, or business by clicking the "Like" link.

- ▶ Buy and sell stuff in the Facebook Marketplace.

- ▶ Share a résumé, or find an employer or an employee.

- ▶ Collaborate on project info at work or school.

- ▶ Market yourself, your products, or your company.

This list is just the tip of the iceberg. There's plenty more to do and see, and plenty of people to meet. So what are you waiting for? Log on and start socializing!

Tour the Facebook Site

The Facebook makers have kept the site fairly simple, which is a major part of its appeal. Naysayers complain that it does not have enough customizing options; but truthfully, most customizing that takes place on personal web pages these days usually ends up making the pages distracting and difficult to follow. Navigationally, Facebook includes a login page as the starting point for entering the website. After you pass that, you're presented with a Home page, shown in Figure 1.1, and links to other pages and features. At the top of every page, you can find a blue navigation bar with links to the Home page (which is always your starting point at every visit), your personal profile page, a link for finding friends, and the Account menu. If you click the **Account** menu, which is basically an unlabeled drop-down arrow that displays a menu of options, you can access settings, the Help Center, and a log out option.

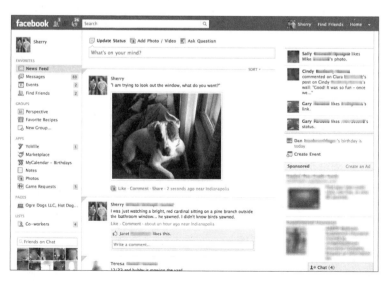

FIGURE 1.1   Here's an example of a Home page on Facebook, where a scrolling news feed appears, along with advertisements and other bits of information.

The left pane area of the page offers more links to Facebook features, such as messages, friends, and groups. The left pane also keeps a running list of friends currently logged in at the same time as you. The right pane lists events and notifications, such as upcoming events, and sponsored advertising. If you scroll to the bottom of any Facebook page, you'll find links for advertisers, developers, terms of service, help, and more.

The Home page is similar to a Grand Central Station for news about your friends on Facebook. It tracks the ongoing status updates of your friends, published photos and videos, shared links, fan pages they've joined, and so forth. All the activities come together on a scrollable page that's constantly changing. The inset ticker area lists up-to-the minute trivial activity, such as game postings and pages "liked." The Home page is where you go to see and be seen on Facebook.

As mentioned previously, the focus in Facebook is on profile pages—the place where you add information about yourself to share with others. Figure 1.2 shows an example of a profile page featuring the new timeline format. A typical profile page includes a picture, a wide cover photo across the top of the page, a status text box so you can let the rest of the Facebook world know what you're up to or what you're thinking, a timeline of activities you're pursuing and postings from friends, and links for accessing other pages and features. For example, to add or edit profile information, you can click the **Update Info** button to view your details and make changes.

In addition to your own page, you can view your friends' profile pages to check out their latest updates and any Facebook activities they're pursuing online. The information you see listed on your Facebook pages is always changing based on your activities and the activities of your friends, so be sure to refresh your pages often.

So far, I've described just a few of the pages you'll encounter. There are many more. Now that you've had a brief tour, you're ready to jump in, right? If you haven't created an account yet, Lesson 2, "Setting Up a Facebook Account," shows you how. If you're already a Facebook member, move on to the other lessons detailing how to use the site and get the most out of your social networking experience. Enjoy!

FIGURE 1.2   Here's an example of a profile page on Facebook.

Summary

In this lesson, you learned about social networking sites and how
Facebook got its start. You also learned about some of the various things
you can do on the site and what to expect when you start viewing pages on
the website. In the next lesson, you learn how to sign up for a Facebook
account and start building your own timeline.

LESSON 2

Setting Up a Facebook Account

In this lesson, you learn how to sign up for a Facebook account, create a timeline, and specify a current status. This information covers everything you need to get started as a Facebook member.

Signing Up for an Account

If you're new to Facebook, the first thing you need to do is sign up for an account. Joining Facebook is free, and the only requirements are that you have a working email address—in other words, a real email address—and you must be 13 years of age or older. At the end of the registration process, Facebook sends you a confirmation email you must follow to finish setting up your account. The process is relatively painless and fast.

NOTE: If you want to create a professional account, such as a profile page for a band or business, you can click the **Create a Page for a celebrity, band or business** link located on the Facebook Sign Up page (see Figure 2.1). Learn more about the professional and promotional sides of Facebook in Lesson 14, "Understanding Pages."

When creating a Facebook account, you need to use your real name. The whole social networking architecture of the site is built on the authenticity of its users. Odd nicknames, pseudonyms, or aliases are simply not allowed. In fact, if you try to use an odd-looking name, it will probably be flagged by Facebook as a possible bogus account. For example, if you attempt to create an account for Lone Ranger, chances are it will not make it. If the name happens to be your real, honest-to-goodness name, you can appeal to Facebook by clicking the **Help** link on the Sign Up page.

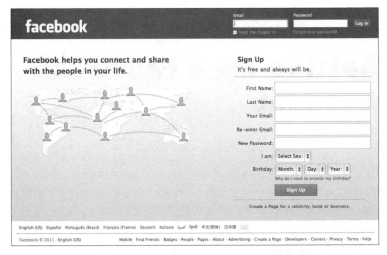

FIGURE 2.1   Facebook's Sign Up page is the place to start when you want to create a new account, as well as where you log in to use your account.

To sign up for an account, follow these steps:

1. Use your web browser to display the Facebook Sign Up page, www.facebook.com.

2. You can start the registration process by filling out the initial sign-up form, shown in Figure 2.1. Click inside the first form box and type your first name.

3. Type in your last name.

4. Type in your email address, and then type it again to confirm that it's correct as originally entered.

5. Establish a password. As with most passwords you use on the Internet, choose one that contains both numbers and letters for maximum security.

6. Click the **I am** field and select your gender.

7. Click the **Birthday** fields to specify your date of birth. Don't worry—you don't have to show this on your profile page if you don't want to. This information is a security measure to make sure you're old enough to use the site.

NOTE: If you already have a Facebook account, you can use the login fields at the top of the page to enter your email and password to log in.

8. Click the **Sign Up** button when you're ready to continue.

9. The next phase of the registration process is the security check, shown in Figure 2.2. Type in the words shown on the screen.

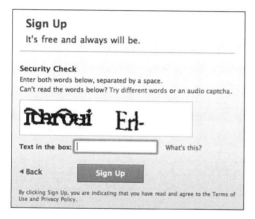

FIGURE 2.2 The Security Check screen verifies you're legit and not auto-mated software trying to create an account.

TIP: If you have difficulty reading the wavy words on the Security Check page, you can click the option for changing the words to a new set or listening to an audio file instead.

10. Click the **Sign Up** button to continue.

NOTE: As you can imagine, people rarely read the terms of service and privacy policy when signing up for things. In case you were wondering, Facebook's policies basically say you're not allowed to send spam or post pirated material, and you're expected to be honest and nice to everyone online. They also say you cannot hold Facebook accountable if you get into trouble. See Lesson 3, "Finding Help with Facebook Services and Etiquette," to learn more about these terms.

The next phase is to add details to your Facebook account. You'll actually go through three main sections, and each page asks you to do something, such as look up friends using your email contacts, specify profile info about your education or job, and add a profile picture. You can choose to pursue each page's options right then and there and add all the necessary details, or you can skip the steps and fill in the information at a later time (or not at all, if you prefer). We'll opt for supplying this information later. Keep in mind that Facebook may change its sign-up steps from time to time, so your own steps might vary slightly.

In Figure 2.3, the first thing Facebook wants to know is whether you want to look up friends by searching through your contacts list and seeing whether any matches already have Facebook accounts. You can learn all about how to find friends in Lesson 6, "Connecting with Friends." For now, just click the **Skip this Step** link at the bottom of the page to continue onward. If you do opt to find friends now, click **Find Friends** and follow the instructions. You can click the **Save & Continue** button to proceed to the next step.

FIGURE 2.3   Step 1 allows you to search for existing friends on Facebook using your email contacts list.

Figure 2.4 shows the second step. This time, Facebook wants to get you started on your profile by adding educational or job information. You can take the time to fill this out now, or you can do so later. Skip this section by clicking the **Skip** link and move on. If you did fill out the info, click **Save & Continue** instead.

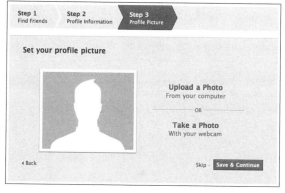

FIGURE 2.4   The second step lets you specify your education and/or work associations.

The third step, shown in Figure 2.5, prompts you to add a profile picture. You can click the **Upload a Photo** option, or if your computer has a web camera, you can click **Take a Photo** and create a new picture. You can also save this task for later and just click the **Skip** link. If you added a picture, click **Save & Continue**.

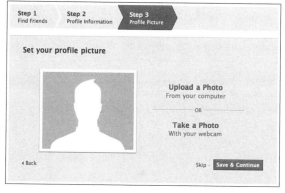

FIGURE 2.5   The third step lets you add a profile picture.

After you jump through all the registration and setup hoops, Facebook finally shows you a customized Welcome page featuring your name (see Figure 2.6). The first thing you need to do is confirm your email address as prompted at the top of the page; go check your email. Facebook sends you an email confirmation. When you open the email message, click the link or cut and paste it into your browser to finish the registration process.

FIGURE 2.6   The Welcome page prompts you to confirm your email address.

CAUTION: Depending on your browser setup, the confirmation process may cause several of the same Facebook pages to open. Use the newest window and close the others as needed.

Now that you have an account, you can begin customizing your profile, adding to your timeline, searching for people you know, adding your mobile device, and so on. The next section shows you how to add nitty-gritty data to your page.

By the way, now that you're officially a member, you can log out and in again using your email address and password at the main Facebook page. You'll see boxes (form fields) at the top of the page to enter both these pertinent pieces of information. You can even tell the site to remember you so you don't have to keep typing in the info each time. As for logging out, you can click the **Account** menu and click **Log Out** to exit the site at any time.

NOTE: New to Facebook, the timeline format on your profile page lists your postings chronologically on an actual timeline that runs down the center of the page. You can add important events to the timeline, such as the birth of a child, graduation, or a new job, to document your life experiences. You can also post regular items to the timeline, such as status updates about what you're currently doing or thinking. The timeline replaces what was formerly known as the wall.

Building Your Profile Page

After you've registered on Facebook and navigated the Getting Started pages, you can start customizing your personal profile right away. A *profile* is just a collection of information about you, such as your hobbies and interests, where you go to school or work, favorite music or television shows, favorite quote, and so on. Your Facebook profile is visible to your friends and anyone on your network. After you complete the registration process, Facebook starts you out with a bare-bones page featuring the new timeline format. It's up to you to add the meat.

In the land of Facebook, *profiles* are for individuals but *pages* are for bands, celebrities, politicians, businesses, and other groups. We focus on your individual profile in this lesson. To see your profile, just click your name link located in the navigation bar at the top of any Facebook page. You'll open a page similar to Figure 2.7.

To learn how to add to your profile, see the next section.

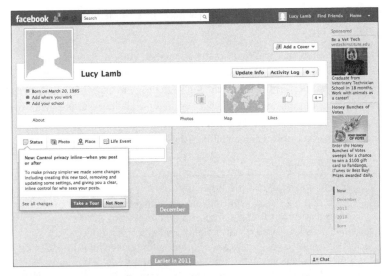

FIGURE 2.7   The bare-bones profile page.

NOTE: A help area, which offers you tips on what to do, might appear on your screen from time to time as you work with your new profile; click **Close** to hide the feature, or follow the directions to learn more about a feature.

Adding to Your Profile Info

Ready to start filling out your profile information? You can click the **About** link located under your profile name area on your page, or you can click the **Update Info** button under the Cover photo area. With either method, Facebook takes you to a page where you can edit your profile's different categories, shown in Figure 2.8. You decide what you want to input. You can choose to make a comprehensive profile, or just dole out little bits of information about yourself. As you can see in Figure 2.8, profile info is grouped into several categories, as follows:

▶ **Work and Education**—This category includes fields for listing your education and employment information, such as which school you attend, where you work, degrees earned, and so on.

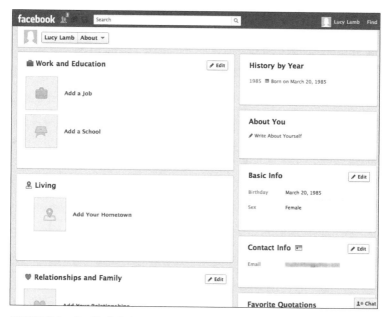

FIGURE 2.8 Profile info is grouped into categories.

▶ **Living**—You can add your hometown here.

▶ **Relationships and Family**—Use this category to set a personal status, such as single or married, and list family members in your profile text.

▶ **About You**—You can add a brief paragraph about yourself using this field.

▶ **Basic Info**—You can change your birthday and gender, relationship status, religious and political views, and other basic info under this category.

▶ **Favorite Quotations**—Open this category to include a favorite quotation on your page.

▶ **Contact Info**—Use this category to input information about how to contact you, such as address, cell phone number, website, and so on.

You can click the **Edit** button for any category to display additional fields for entering data or selecting options. Some fields are text boxes; others are drop-down menus with selections you make. You may notice as you type that Facebook tries to help you with common words and phrases in a pop-up box that appears. You can make selections from the pop-up box and insert them immediately, or you can just ignore the suggestions and keep on typing.

As you make changes to the data in each category, you must click the **Save** button at the bottom of the form to keep your changes.

When you have finished filling out the profile information, you can click your name button at the top of the page to return to the normal profile page view.

> TIP: If you have an account with an instant messaging service, you can add your screen name or alias to your Facebook page using the Contact Info category options.

Adding a Profile Picture

You can add a picture to your profile to help people recognize you. Facebook uses your picture as an *avatar*, an image that represents you as you interact with other profiles, groups, and so forth. You can also add a cover photo to your page to add visual interest, but you'll learn more about this in Lesson 4, "Navigating Your Timeline." If you already added a profile picture when setting up your account, you can skip this section. If you haven't added a picture yet, stick around.

If you have a digital image of yourself stored on your computer, you can quickly add it for all to see. If you don't have a portrait photo readily available, you can also insert another type of picture that represents you, such as a picture of your favorite hobby, sport, or pet. A profile picture can be up to 4MB in file size.

You can choose to upload a picture already stored on your computer or, if your computer has a built-in camera, you can take a new picture to use. If you've previously added photos to your Facebook account, a third option appears for choosing from your existing photos.

Let's focus on using a picture already stored on your computer. To get started, you can click on any of the **Upload a Photo** links you see on your pages wherever you encounter them (such as the Welcome page for new users). Any time you want to update or change your picture from the profile page, simply move the mouse pointer over the picture area until an **Edit Profile Picture** menu appears, as shown in Figure 2.9. Click it and choose how you want to add a photo.

FIGURE 2.9   You can add a photo directly from your profile page.

Inevitably, all uploading tasks lead to an Open dialog box. You've seen this dialog box hundreds of times in other programs on your computer; use it to navigate to the file you want and double-click to open the file and start the uploading process. Depending on your Internet connection speed and the size of the file, the process may take a second or several minutes. When it's done, however, your picture appears. Figure 2.10 shows an uploaded photo added. Notice the new addition is also duly noted on your timeline.

TIP: You can add more than one profile picture to your account and switch between them as the mood strikes you. Facebook stores your profile pictures in the Profile Picture album. Click the Photos near the top of your profile page, and click the Profile Pictures album to view, edit, and add new pics.

NOTE: You can now create your own personal URL to your Facebook profile page using a unique username. This feature is handy if you want to direct people directly to your page. To create a Facebook URL, follow this link to set it up: www.facebook.com/*username*.

FIGURE 2.10   The newly uploaded picture appears.

Changing Your Status

There's one more task you can do to help you start your Facebook experience—add a status update. You can use your status posting to share a thought, tell people what you're doing at the current moment, or mention other points of interest. Anything you post in the "What's on your mind?" box appears in the news feeds of your friends, as well as on your own timeline. The first time you use this feature, Facebook offers a help tutorial, as shown in Figure 2.11. You can use the self-guided tutorial to learn about the feature. Just follow the on-screen prompts.

To change your status, follow these steps:

1. Click in the **What's on your mind?** box and type an entry.

2. Click the **Post** button.

Facebook adds the posting to your timeline (see Figure 2.12). Others can now respond with a comment.

FIGURE 2.11 You can update your status to let people know what you're thinking or what you're doing.

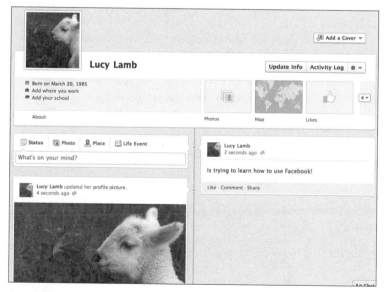

FIGURE 2.12 Facebook adds the new status to your timeline.

When you start typing in the status box, additional options appear above the box and more option icons appear directly below the box. You can use the top options to include a photo, designate a place, or a life event. You can use the bottom options to specify a friend, date, or location. Over next to the Post button is an option that lets you control who sees the status update. By default, the status is viewable by everyone on Facebook unless you change the privacy setting. To change it, click the button and choose a setting, such as **Friends**. You can learn more about these settings in Lesson 7, "Guarding Your Privacy."

> TIP: Need to remove your status? Move your mouse pointer over the status listing and click the button that appears in the upper-right corner of the post. A menu appears; click the Remove Post option.

Accessing Your Account Info

You can always access your Facebook account info to make changes to your email address, name (if you get married, for example), password, and other settings. To do so, move your mouse pointer over the **Account** menu at the top of the Facebook page (looks like a drop-down arrow), and then click **Account Settings** from the drop-down menu.

The Account Settings page appears, as shown in Figure 2.13. To change any account information, click the Edit link for the data you want to edit, and then make the appropriate changes. Be sure to click the **Save Changes** button to keep your edits.

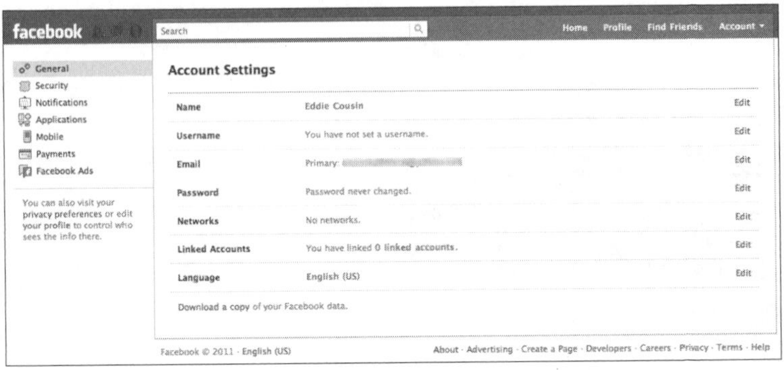

FIGURE 2.13   The Account Settings page lets you change basic account details.

To return to your profile page again, click your name button on the navigation bar at the top of the Facebook page.

TIP: Learn more about changing account settings, such as privacy settings, in Lesson 7. Learn how to control notification settings in Lesson 5.

Summary

In this lesson, you learned how to sign up for a Facebook account and how to begin building your profile page, including adding information and a photo. You also learned how to update your status and access your account information. In the next lesson, you learn how to use Facebook's Help Center and find some tips about how to conduct yourself on the website.

LESSON 3

Finding Help with Facebook Services and Etiquette

In this lesson, you learn about Facebook's terms of service, what to expect with the social do's and don'ts of using Facebook, and how to find help with the website.

Understanding Facebook's Terms of Service

Facebook operates under the guidance of a set of values, goals, and rules for how the site works and how users interact. These guidelines are important for the general well-being of its members and for the smooth and seamless functioning of the site. When you sign up for Facebook, you're agreeing to uphold and follow their terms of service. If you're like most people, however, you didn't take the time to read all the legalese and fine print. In a nutshell, the terms of service are broken down into several categories, such as privacy, information sharing, safety, account security, and topics along those lines.

You can read the terms yourself by scrolling to the bottom of any Facebook page and clicking the **Terms** link. The link always sits at the bottom of a page, along with links to Facebook's Help Center page and privacy principles. When you click the **Terms** link, Facebook opens a page detailing a statement of rights and responsibilities, as shown in Figure 3.1.

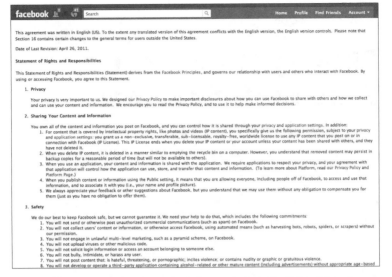

FIGURE 3.1   Facebook's terms of service page featuring fine print and legalese.

You can certainly take time to read all the fine print, but if you just want a quick overview, here are a few details about the terms:

▶ **Privacy**—Facebook promises to do its best to keep your information private or at least disclose to you if it shares it with others. Controlling your own privacy settings, however, is up to you. (Learn more about changing privacy settings in Lesson 7, "Guarding Your Privacy.")

▶ **Sharing content and information**—You're the owner of the content and information you post on Facebook. However, by posting it, you're giving Facebook permission to use any content covered by intellectual property rights (kind of a license to use the content until you cancel your account).

NOTE: Keep in mind that if you delete content or even your entire Facebook account, much of that content still resides somewhere on the servers, including content shared with others. For this reason, do not post content that you do not want others to access or control.

▶ **Safety**—Under this broad category, you cannot collect information from other users, send spam, upload viruses, solicit login information from others, bully other users, or use Facebook for illegal purposes. In other words, behave yourself.

▶ **Content**—You cannot post content that is hateful or threatening to others. You cannot post pornographic material, or nudity of any kind. You're also not allowed to post anything featuring gratuitous violence. This terms of service category is basically about using common sense and being a good citizen, conducting yourself in a way that would make your parents proud.

▶ **Account security**—You cannot supply Facebook with false or outdated information, and keeping your password safe is up to you, to prevent unauthorized access. You cannot use Facebook if you're under 13 years of age. You cannot use Facebook if you're in a country that is currently under embargo. If you're a convicted sex offender, you're not allowed on Facebook.

So what happens if you violate the terms of service? Facebook has the right to terminate your account for any misdeeds, misconduct, illegal activities, and so forth. It can remove questionable content you post if it violates the terms of service. Basically, you'll get in trouble if you don't play nicely with others. Most of us learned this concept early on. However, there's always someone out there looking for trouble. If you encounter such a person, you can report him or her on Facebook (as discussed more fully in Lesson 7).

If you're interested in reading more about Facebook's privacy policies, such as exactly what information is collected from you and shared, click the **Privacy** link at the bottom of any Facebook page. You can also get to the page by clicking the **Privacy Policy** link found amid the terms of service information.

As with many large-scale websites, Facebook's terms and privacy policies change over time. You can always revisit the terms of service and principles pages to read up on the most current rules and regulations.

Facebook Etiquette

As you can probably guess, anytime you throw together a bunch of people from diverse backgrounds, ages, experiences, political leanings, religions, and computer proficiency, things happen—expectations differ, assumptions are made, worlds collide. As with interacting in the real world, interacting in the online world takes some skill and diplomacy. Sure, you might have joined Facebook just to have fun with your friends, but maybe your version of fun differs from the people you have assembled on your Friends list. So what are the social do's and don'ts of using Facebook?

There's no real guide to interacting other than your own common sense and intuition. As in real life, in online life, the golden rule still applies: Treat others as you want to be treated. If you're looking for a few tips anyway, here they are.

Facebook Do's

▶ Do be tolerant of others, particularly when you get friend requests from people you don't immediately recognize or know. They may be looking for someone with the same name. If you don't want to respond, just ignore the request.

▶ Do set your privacy settings to the levels in which you feel comfortable and safe. By default, many of the privacy settings are set for everyone to see your profile information and other postings. Adjusting these settings to include just your friends is a good idea. (See Lesson 7 to learn more about Facebook settings.)

▶ Do report threatening behavior or inappropriate postings. Facebook takes this sort of thing very seriously. You can visit the Help Center page to find a report feature.

▶ Do be considerate of other people's feelings. Communicating electronically is often a challenge because people can't see your face or hear the tone of your voice. Remember this when posting on timelines and making comments. On the other hand, don't fly off the handle when you're not sure what someone else means—misinterpreting someone else's remarks is dangerously easy online.

▶ Do reply to comments and personal messages when applicable. At least acknowledging people who attempt to communicate with you is mannerly.

▶ Do keep your postings civil and free of foul or questionable language. Remember, that person's other friends see your comments (perhaps even that person's mother).

▶ Do choose an appropriate profile picture. Tacky or questionable pictures are not the way to go unless that's really the message you want to convey to friends, family, coworkers, or your boss.

▶ Do use your head about what information you share on Facebook and how you conduct yourself. With regard to the issue of saying too much online, let discretion be your first instinct. Saying too little is always better than saying too much.

Facebook Don'ts

▶ Don't think of your Friends list as a competition to see who has the most. It's not. Quality over quantity is the best approach. If you're sending friend requests right and left to people you don't intend to know, you're in this for the wrong reasons.

▶ Don't give out your personal information unless you really know the person. When you do share personal information, do so via private email messages, not the public forum that is the Facebook timeline. Always be cautious about sharing personal or confidential information—never give out your information to someone you don't know.

▶ Don't irritate people with your postings. Keep in mind that not everyone wants to hear about your adorable pet rabbit, Fluffy, every single hour of every single day.

▶ Don't annoy people with too many "pokes" or other application actions. It's fun the first time, but over and over again all day is too much. (See Lesson 13, "Adding Applications," to learn more about applications.)

▶ Don't use Facebook as a tool for revenge, bullying, or threats. Such activities will get you kicked off faster than a speeding bullet.

▶ Don't feel obligated to befriend everyone on Facebook. If you don't want a particular person snooping around your profile, you can deny his or her friend request.

▶ Don't share company information online—that's a big no-no.

▶ Don't make your romantic break-ups and get-togethers public knowledge. Save that sort of information for private forums and messaging.

▶ Don't lower your guard just because you're with "friends" on Facebook. Accounts can be hijacked, and shared links can take you to questionable places or encourage you to download files that turn out to be viruses or malware.

Finding Help with the Help Center

You may encounter times in which you need a little extra help with your Facebook experience—for example, if you're having a technical issue with your account or want to know more about a particular feature. Check out the Facebook Help Center for answers. Among the help offerings are video tutorials, articles, discussion forums, and other resources. The Help Center, shown in Figure 3.2, is just a click away. To view the page, click the **Help** link at the bottom of any Facebook page. You can also click the drop-down arrow on the navigation bar at the top of the page and click **Help** from the drop-down menu that appears.

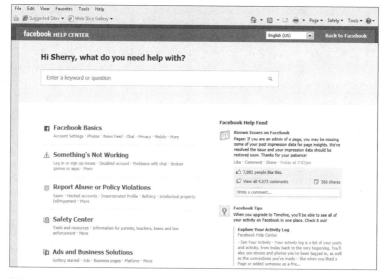

FIGURE 3.2 Visit Facebook's Help Center page when you need help.

The Help Center page organizes content into several categories, as outlined here:

▶ **Facebook Basics**—Lists topics for Facebook usage, such as Account Settings, how to work with photos, chat, mobile devices, and so on.

▶ **Something's Not Working**—Lists topics for all kinds of issues you might have with the website, such as logon problems, disabled accounts, apps not working properly, and so on.

▶ **Report Abuse or Policy Violations**—Lists links to help you report spam, hacked accounts, cyber-bullying, and more.

▶ **Safety Center**—Lists links to learn more about tools and resources, important information for parents and teachers, and other tips.

▶ **Ads and Business Solutions**—Lists topics for advertisers, businesses, and developers for using the Facebook site.

Click a category to view more links.

To read more about a topic, just click it to open a page with more details. If you don't find the answer you're looking for, try clicking another topic.

To look up a topic, click in the **Search** box at the top of the Help Center page, type in the word or phrase you want to look up, and press **Enter** (or **Return**) or click the **Search** button.

If you're looking for an exchange of information from other users in a discussion-style setting, click the **Community Forum** link. You'll find it on the Help Center page near the bottom. It opens a page where you can post a question and have it answered by other users (see Figure 3.3). You can browse through posted questions and review answers, find links to top questions, and more.

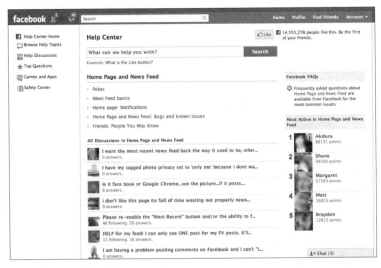

FIGURE 3.3   You can get personalized help on the Facebook community forums where you can post questions and view answers from other users.

If you need help with games and apps, click the **Games and Apps** link at the bottom of the Help Center page. As with the community forums, it opens a page listing help links for various games and apps you are using that have been created by other developers. The links take you to the app's developer page for more information.

TIP: If you're still having trouble finding help, try one of the many Facebook-centric blogs outside of Facebook, including http://blog.facebook.com or www.allfacebook.com. If you're an advertiser on Facebook, the Inside Facebook blog is worth checking out at www.insidefacebook.com. If you're having a technical issue, try the People-Powered Customer Service for Facebook board at http://getsatisfaction.com/facebook.

Summary

In this lesson, you learned about Facebook's terms of service, a few tips for following proper social networking etiquette, and how to find help in times of trouble using Facebook's Help Center pages. In the next lesson, you learn more about navigating your profile, including instructions on how to use the new timeline.

Navigating Your Timeline

In this lesson, you learn how to utilize all the different elements of your timeline page, formerly known as a profile. You'll learn how to navigate your way around the new timeline, change your profile picture and cover picture, post status updates, and more.

Timeline Basics

New to Facebook, the timeline is an evolution of the old profile page of just a profile photo and a list of interests into a visual account of your ongoing story. Whether you still call it a profile or a timeline, it's basically still a page containing information about you.

In past renditions of Facebook, the profile page included an area called the *Wall* in which you and your friends could post comments, stories, photos, links, and other shared information. The Wall was a fairly obvious area in the middle of the page where the newest items were listed on top and older items eventually dropped off the page as new items were added. With the new timeline format, everything is plugged into a vertical line of time, hence the word *timeline*, running down the center of the page. You can visually see when each story item was added and the progression of activities across the span of time. This new format makes it easy to jump back and view past events. You can even add key events into the timeline, even though the actual date has passed. Stories are organized by year, and on the far-right side of the page is a year-based timeline where you can click a year and view your stories for that particular year.

Your timeline actually consists of several key elements. You've already learned about several of those elements in the process of creating an account, such as your profile picture. Now it's time to go into a little more detail. After you start adding friends, liking pages, adding apps, and other Facebook activities, your page starts looking more like the one shown in Figure 4.1.

FIGURE 4.1   Here's a typical timeline page.

To help you make sense of the new timeline, let's take a look at the main areas of the page. The top of the page, right below the blue navigation bar, displays a large customizable photo called the *cover*, with an inset profile picture. The cover photo offers you a way to uniquely customize your page with a large visual element.

Below the cover and profile picture is your name and a bit of the information you added when you set up your account, such as birthday, education, or employer. If you didn't add any info yet, the areas here appear as links that you can click and then fill in the necessary info.

Next to your name is a bar area featuring buttons that take you to your About page for filling in or changing info, to your Activity Log detailing your activities, and a drop-down menu of other settings.

Also in the top area of the page, below the cover, are boxes featuring several unique apps that work within the Facebook framework, each with a particular focus. Included in this area:

- ▶ **Friends**—Click here to see a list of all the friends you've added on Facebook.

- ▶ **Photos**—Open the Photos apps to add photos and videos, create albums, and view photos in which others have tagged you.

- ▶ **Map**—This application tracks all the places you've been, lived, visited, and more.

- ▶ **Likes**—This app lists your favorite things and interests, along with Pages you like.

- ▶ **Notes**—This app keeps all your notes and blog entries.

- ▶ **Subscriptions**—This feature lets you subscribe to other news streams without actually adding them as friends, such as celebrities, journalists, and other interesting people.

As you add more apps, this area of the page grows.

The next section of the page is where the actual timeline begins, as shown in Figure 4.2. A fresh status update box awaits your input at the top of the timeline. Over on the right, a Friends box features a random sampling of your Facebook friends. Below that is an area listing your recent activities, such as Pages you liked, people you've subscribed to, and friends you just made.

The rest of the screen unfolds in stories listed in month-based sections. Newer stories appear at the top of the screen.

Off on the right side of the screen are sponsored ads along with a yearly graph of your longevity on Facebook. You can click a year to view the stories recorded during that time.

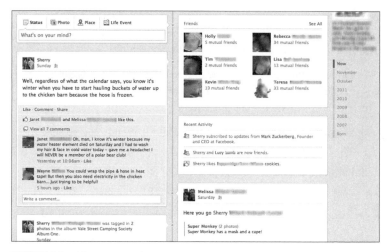

FIGURE 4.2   The middle of the page starts the actual timeline area.

Adding a Cover Photo

As mentioned previously, the cover photo is an opportunity to give your page visual impact. You can use a cover image to personalize the page, such as showcasing a favorite day, hobby, or interest, or just decorate your page with something visually appealing. You may want to feature a different photo for different seasons or months, or just keep the same picture forever. It's totally up to you. Facebook stores all the cover photos in a folder named Cover Photos, which you can find among the other albums kept by the Photos app.

To add or change the cover, click anywhere on the cover to display a Change Cover menu, shown in Figure 4.3. Click the drop-down arrow button and select whether you want to use a previously uploaded photo or upload a new photo. Select the photo you want to use. When Facebook has the photo placed, you can drag it to reposition it however it best suits the wide cover area, as shown in Figure 4.4. When everything is to your liking, click the **Save Changes** button.

FIGURE 4.3   You can change your cover photo as often as you want.

FIGURE 4.4   You can drag your photo to reposition it in the cover area.

If the cover photo needs adjusting, you can click the **Change Cover** drop-down menu again and select **Reposition**.

To remove the photo entirely, open the menu and select **Remove**. When you remove the cover image, a blank placeholder appears in its place.

Changing Your Profile Picture

To change your profile photo, move the mouse pointer over the inset picture and click the **Edit Profile Picture** drop-down arrow. Facebook displays a menu of options, as shown in Figure 4.5. You can choose another photo from previously uploaded pictures, take a new photo with your computer's camera, or upload a new photo. For example, to swap your profile picture with another, click the **Choose from Photos** option to open the Choose from Your

Photos box, shown in Figure 4.6, and select a different profile picture to post. Profile pictures are stored in an album called, appropriately, Profile Pictures.

FIGURE 4.5 Swapping out your profile picture with another photo is easy.

FIGURE 4.6 Look through your albums for a picture to use, or open the Profile Pictures album.

If the profile picture photo needs adjusting, you can click the **Edit Profile Picture** drop-down menu again and select **Edit Thumbnail**. This opens the Edit Thumbnail dialog box, shown in Figure 4.7, and you can adjust the photo to get just the right fit. Click **Save** to save your changes.

FIGURE 4.7   Use this dialog box to reposition your profile picture.

To remove the photo entirely, open the Edit Profile Picture menu and select **Remove**. This option removes the picture and leaves a generic placeholder image in its place.

Viewing Your Activity Log

The Activity Log keeps chronological track of your daily activities all the way back to when you first joined Facebook. No one else can see or access your log. You can use the log to review and manage your stories and other bits of information shared on Facebook. The log keeps track of activities such as when you change a profile picture to when you commented on someone else's photo. To access the log, click the **Activity Log** button under the cover photo on your timeline page. Figure 4.8 shows a typical Activity Log page.

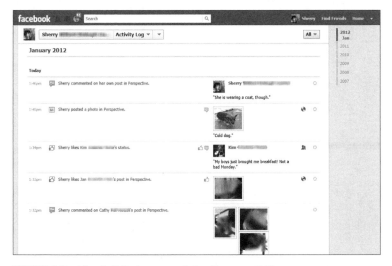

FIGURE 4.8   The Activity Log page lists all your activities.

You can use the All drop-down arrow at the top of the page to filter the types of information displayed in the log. Click the arrow, shown in Figure 4.9, to view the filters and click the one you want to employ. You can use the far-right column next to the item descriptions to control what appears on the timeline or manage posts elsewhere. Click a circle to display a menu of options. For example, you can decide to feature an item so it appears prominently on your timeline, or hide an item altogether. Depending on the item, you can also change the audience selector and allow a customized friends list to view the posting. The activity log even keeps track of who liked or commented on your posts. When you scroll to the bottom of the log page, you can click the **More Activity** link to view more activity.

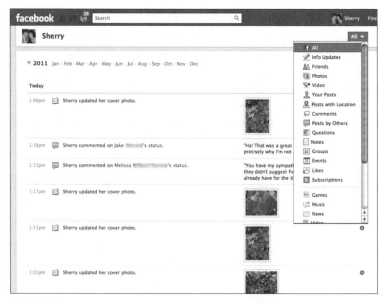

FIGURE 4.9   You can filter the Activity Log using the items on this menu.

NOTE: The top of your Activity Log may show some pending posts in the Profile Review area. This is a privacy option you can use to grant approval to others who tag you. You can manage each request or approve all at once. Click the check mark button to approve a tag post, or click the **Approve All** button to approve everything listed.

Working with Stories

Items you add to your timeline are called *stories*. Stories can be status updates, photos, links you share, and even postings left by your friends. You can add stories at any point in your timeline. You can feature a story with a star icon, allowing you to highlight its importance by making it expand across the timeline. Highlighted stories always appear visible in the timeline. You can also hide stories, control who sees a story, or remove ones you no longer want associated with your timeline.

Updating Your Status

To post something on your own timeline, fill out a status update and share it. Essentially, this creates a story on your page. Click in the text box at the top of your page, as shown in Figure 4.10, where it says something like, "What's on your mind?" In previous versions of the Facebook interface, the box had different titles. The name or text may change at any time, but the intent remains the same: to share something that you're thinking or doing, some random remark, observation, or witty thought. Status updates also include important events and activities in your life, and you can share more than just a blurb or comment.

FIGURE 4.10 Use the status update box to post an update about what you're doing or thinking.

To add a story to your timeline, type out your status update and then press **Enter** (**Return**) or click the **Post** button to post it on your page. Facebook adds the information to your timeline, as well as to the news feed that appears on the Home page.

TIP: You can also fill out the update box on your Home page to update your Facebook status. When you click in the box, additional buttons appear for adding photos, a video, or a polling question.

The update box is technically known as the *Publisher.* When you activate the **What's on your mind?** box, which you can do just by clicking inside the field, you can use the additional buttons above the field for sharing:

► **Status**—The default selection, this simply adds a regular post about what you're thinking or doing.

► **Photo**—Choose this option to add or include a photo in your posting.

► **Place**—You can use this feature to map a location for the story, such as a coffee shop or city.

► **Life Event**—Use this feature to mark a specific type of event in your life, such as a new job, hobby, or engagement.

You can also tag people in your story. Click the tag icon (the first gray icon beneath the update box) to type in a specific person's name. You can click the date icon (the second gray icon) to tag a year with the posting. You might do this when sharing an old photo, for example. To add a location to the post, you can click the location icon (the third gray icon) and type in a location.

To set a specific audience for the post, such as only viewed by a customized group of friends, click the **Audience Selector** drop-down arrow next to the **Post** button and choose a different privacy setting.

How often you update your status is entirely up to you. It really depends on how often you log in to Facebook and how much you want to share about what you're doing or thinking. Some users prefer to post updates several times a day; others prefer to post more sporadically based on things that happen throughout their day. Other users choose to update their status once a day or, if feeling not so social, once a week. Facebook stories are really all about connecting and sharing with your friends, so deciding how much to participate and share is up to you.

TIP: You can highlight a posted story so it's featured across the entire page, making it more prominent. To do so, move the mouse pointer over the posting's top-right corner and click the **Star** icon that appears. You can click the icon again to remove the feature status.

Posting on a Friend's Timeline

You can visit a friend's timeline and add a story. When you view her page, you'll see the same Update Status box found on your own page. Click in it and type up your post. You can also use the box to add a photo, a video, tag another person, or tag a particular location, just as you can with your own status updates. When you finish typing, click the **Share** button or press **Enter** (**Return**).

Removing a Post

Sometimes you might need to edit your timeline postings. For example, you may need to correct a spelling or remove a questionable post someone left on your page. To delete a post from the timeline, move your mouse pointer over the post and click the **Edit or Remove** icon that appears in the upper-right corner of the post. Select **Delete Post** from the menu that appears. Facebook displays a prompt box, shown in Figure 4.11. Click **Delete Post** to remove the post entirely.

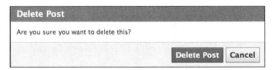

FIGURE 4.11   Facebook displays this prompt box when you try to delete a post.

You can also remove a post you left on a friend's timeline. Open your Activity Log page as described earlier in this lesson; then click the circle icon at the far-right side of the post and select **Delete Post**. You can also visit the person's timeline page and use the same deletion technique for removing your own posts. In other words, your ability to remove posts is limited to your own posts (wherever they are) and anything on your timeline; you can't delete other people's posts from their timelines.

Summary

In this lesson, you learned how to navigate and manage your timeline page, and work with Facebook stories. In the next lesson, you learn how to use the Home page.

LESSON 5

Navigating the Home Page

In this lesson, you learn how to keep track of news and activities on Facebook. You'll learn how information flows on the site, and how to use the Home page to view the news feed and notifications to keep abreast of the latest information.

Understanding Facebook Information Flow

As a social networking site, Facebook acts much like a broadcasting service, sharing news about its members wherever they are. However, rather than tuning in to see general news about everyone on the site or stories selected entirely by Facebook, your news is narrowed down to just the people you know—your friends, family, coworkers, or colleagues. The news that is shared—whether it's status updates, photos, or the latest link someone posted—is referred to as *stories* on Facebook. This news is also called *feed stories*, *stream*, or *news feed* stories. The information that appears on the Home page is a constant stream of stories about the activities and pursuits of your friends. The official name for this is *news feed*, so that's what we'll call it, too. The stories that appear on your profile's timeline are *mini-feeds* because they're all about you.

For example, anytime you post a status update on your profile page, it's a story on your timeline—mini-feed information dedicated to you. When your friend shares a photo, it appears on his timeline as a mini-feed about him. Out on the Home page, both stories may appear listed as news feed stories where other friends you both know can see them.

What exactly constitutes as news on Facebook, you may wonder? Anything you do on the site is considered a story. If you comment on someone's timeline, for example, or share a link, it appears as an activity, and potentially listed in the main news feed. If you don't want to share all your Facebook activities, you can turn off some of this through your privacy settings. (See Lesson 7, "Guarding Your Privacy," to learn more.)

Another part of this ongoing stream of broadcasting is a Facebook feature called *notifications*. Notifications are messages from Facebook telling you about something that happened on Facebook involving you somehow, such as being tagged (pointed out) in a photo or if someone wrote on your wall. Typically, these notifications are emailed to you or sent via your mobile connection. On Facebook, they appear on the Notifications pop-up list or in the left pane of the Home page. Unlike mini-feeds that are generated by you, or news feeds that detail the activities of others, notifications involve you indirectly.

Let's get down to the nitty-gritty details of how to navigate and work with info on the Home page.

Understanding the Home Page

The Home page is where all the Facebook action takes place outside of your profile page. To view the Home page, click **Home** on the navigation bar (the blue bar at the top of any Facebook page). A page similar to Figure 5.1 appears. Not only do you see a news feed of recent items, the page also includes links to other features, both on the left and right panes of the page, plus some discreet advertising and a visual listing of who's online.

Top and center on the Home page is another status update box, labeled Update Status. This is the same box you use to post status updates to your profile page. (This is just another way of sharing your activity on Facebook without having to redisplay your profile page. To learn more about posting a status update, see Lesson 4, "Navigating Your Timeline.")

Using the Navigation Bar

The navigation bar appears at the top of every Facebook page, with the exception of the Help Center. This blue bar offers several options in addition to the Home button. The left side of the bar, over by the Facebook name, displays three notification icons, shown in Figure 5.2. Click these to open a pop-up list of the latest activity regarding friend requests, messages, or other notifications.

FIGURE 5.1   Here's a typical Home page, showing a news feed in the middle, shortcut links along the left pane, and advertising along the right pane.

FIGURE 5.2   The notification icons display lists of recent Facebook notifications regarding your friends, emails, or game and app requests.

In the center area of the navigation bar is a large box for typing in key-words you want to search for on the site, shown in Figure 5.3. You can use Facebook's Search box to search for friends, professional pages, groups, games, and more. Just click inside the box and start typing. As you type, Facebook automatically tries to guess at what you're searching for and dis-plays a list of possible matches; click a match from the list or click the **See More Results** link at the bottom of the list to open a full page of search results and filters.

FIGURE 5.3   Use the Search box to look for keywords and conduct a search.

Over on the right side of the navigation bar, shown in Figure 5.4, are the following four buttons:

▶ **<Your Name>**—Click your name button to return to your pro-file page.

FIGURE 5.4   The navigation buttons.

▶ **Find Friends**—Visible only to new users, click this button to display the friend options available on Facebook. Learn more about how to locate friends in Lesson 6, "Connecting with Friends."

▶ **Home**—Click this button to open the Home page.

▶ **Account drop-down arrow**—Click this button, also called the Account menu, to view a drop-down menu for accessing account settings, privacy settings, the Facebook Help Center, and a log off command.

Using the Left Pane

Over on the left side of the Home page is a listing of links to popular features and apps, as shown in Figure 5.5. Facebook calls this area a left-hand menu, which isn't a very good name for something so prominent and doesn't really resemble a traditional menu, but oh well. Regardless, you'll find groupings of links that, when clicked, open other pages and features.

FIGURE 5.5   The left column of the Home page lists shortcut links to popular features, apps, groups, and more.

Here's a look at the main categories found in the left pane:

▶ **Favorites**—Lists the most common apps and features.

▶ **Groups**—Lists groups you've joined. To view more groups than can fit in the list, click the **Groups** heading label to open the Groups page. You can learn more about groups in Lesson 11, "Joining Groups."

▶ **Apps**—Lists recent apps you're using. To view more apps, click the **Apps** heading label to open the Apps page with a full listing of everything you've added to your Facebook account. Learn about apps in Lesson 13, "Adding Applications."

▶ **Pages**—Lists recent Pages you've liked. Click the **Pages** heading label to open a page listing all the professional Pages you've added. Learn more about Pages in Lesson 14, "Understanding Pages."

▶ **Lists**—If you've created specialized friends lists in Facebook, they appear here. Click the Lists heading label to view a page of all your lists. Learn how to make customized lists in Lesson 6.

Below the shortcut links you can find a visual display of thumbnails representing every friend who is currently online at the same time as you. Click a friend's picture thumbnail to open a chat box and chat with them. You can learn more about chatting in Lesson 8, "Communicating Through Facebook."

Using the Right Pane Area

Over on the right side of the Home page is another column of info. The top of the column, shown in Figure 5.6, displays a real-time ticker listing what apps, groups, and comments your friends are currently pursuing. The ticker is scrollable, which means you can move your mouse over the area and scroll up and down to view all the action. Click or hover over a ticker item to view more details or join in the conversation.

If you do not see a ticker on your screen, it's probably because you're not using Facebook very much. The feature is only active if there's content to display.

FIGURE 5.6 The right column of the Home page displays a ticker, events, and advertising.

NOTE: If you're playing a game on Facebook, you'll see different activities listed in the ticker on the game page. Instead of regular Facebook actions, you'll see other app activities listed in the ticker.

Below the ticker is a spot announcing the day's events. This includes parties and birthdays, as well as other events you're invited to attend. To view more details about an event, click the event name. You can learn more about events in Lesson 12, "Tracking Events."

Facebook always lists birthdays next to events, so be sure to glance at this area to find out whose birthday it is.

Sponsored ads appear below the events. Ads can range from products and services, popular and obscure, to promotional blurbs about other Facebook groups and professional pages. You can click an ad link to learn more about the product or feature.

NOTE: One of Facebook's enduring apps is the Poke. A form of non-verbal communication, the Poke app lets you "poke" someone digitally as a way to say hello, similar to a gentle punch to the shoulder or nudge to the ribs, all without the need to type in any words. When someone pokes you, it appears as a notification in the right-side pane beneath events.

Working with Your News Feeds

Whenever you want to see what everyone else is doing, click **Home** to display the constantly updating stories, or live stream, that comprise the news feed about your friends and what they're up to on Facebook. The news feed is displayed in the middle of the Home page as a scrollable list of postings (see Figure 5.7). You can read through the news and find out what's happening, view thumbnails of photos, share links, and more.

FIGURE 5.7   The Home page always displays the news feed.

Facebook displays highlighted stories first in the news feed. This is the default sorting filter unless you change it. This simply means any stories you haven't seen yet appear at the top of the page. You can always tell a story is highlighted by the lightly shaded triangle in the upper-left corner of the item. You can click the **Sort** menu found in the top-right corner of the news feed area and choose to view stories in the order they were posted. This second sort option, appropriately called Recent Stories First, lists items in the news feed with the newest items at the top of the page.

You can choose to hide stories that annoy you or that come from people you don't want to see. Move your mouse pointer over the story and look for a drop-down arrow that appears to the right, as shown in Figure 5.8.

FIGURE 5.8   You can control how stories appear in the news feed using the pop-up menu.

Click the arrow to view a menu of options. You can choose to hide the story by selecting **Hide story**. To no longer see any of the stories from that person, select the **Hide all by** command. If you've subscribed to someone's postings, you can use the Unsubscribe commands to turn them off or turn off just the activity stories.

Here are a few more things you can do with the news feed:

▶ Click a person's name in your news feed to immediately open the person's profile page.

▶ Add to the person's story by clicking the **Comment** link and adding a comment.

▶ Rather than type up a comment, click the **Like** link in the story.

▶ Click a photo to view a larger picture.

▶ Click a link to view the associated web page.

▶ Click a video to view a video clip.

▶ Click an application link to add the listed application for yourself.

▶ If you scroll to the bottom of the Home page, you can click the **Older Posts** link to view more stories.

Viewing and Controlling Notifications

As mentioned at the beginning of this lesson, notifications are messages from Facebook to alert you to stories or activities that involve you somehow. If a friend tags you in a note, for example, or joins your group, you'll see a notification. Some applications you use also automatically generate notifications concerning you. You can view a brief listing of notifications by clicking the **Notifications** icon (a globe) in the upper-left corner of the Facebook page (refer to Figure 5.2). The icon often has a red number that pops up next to it, indicating how many notifications you have waiting to be read.

For a full-on display of all your notifications, however, you need to open the Notifications page. Click the **Notifications** icon, and then click **See All Notifications**. This page, similar to Figure 5.9, displays notifications sent from you or received from others.

TIP: You can subscribe to your notifications on Facebook, turning them into an RSS feed (which stands for Really Simple Syndication, formats for web feeds of updated content) that you can read through an RSS reader (such as Google Reader or Bloglines). Just click the RSS link on the Notifications page and follow the instructions.

FIGURE 5.9   You can view all your notifications on the Notifications page.

Notifications are grouped chronologically by date, so today's notifications appear at the top of the page. Depending on the type of notification, you can click a link to read the message. You can easily stop pesky notifications from annoying applications by turning them off. Click the **Notifications Settings** link at the top of the page to find settings for controlling all of your notifications through Facebook.

> NOTE: You can easily confuse notifications with requests, and with some applications, the information may appear in both formats. Notifications focus on notifying you, similar to a mini-news bulletin. Requests focus on inviting you to action, such as befriending someone or joining a group.

Summary

In this lesson, you learned how to navigate the Home page and use the news feed stream to view news about your friends. You also learned how notifications work in Facebook and how to view them. In the next lesson, you learn more about connecting with your friends on Facebook.

LESSON 6

Connecting with Friends

In this lesson, you learn how to use the Facebook Friends features to connect with friends online. You learn how to find friends, respond to friend requests, and view and organize your lists of friends.

Finding Friends

Because you can't really have a social network without friends in some form or fashion, let's get started with learning how to connect with people on Facebook. Many people find themselves invited to join Facebook by their friends who are already online. If this is the case for you, you already have some friend connections to get you started. If you're brand-spanking new to Facebook, you'll have to start finding friends from scratch.

After you start accumulating friends, you'll see their stories posted out on the Home page. This is officially called an *automatic subscription*.

Looking Up Friends

Looking up people on Facebook and establishing online connections is easy. For example, if you want to find an old high school chum or look to see whether a family member has a profile on the site, you can use the Facebook tools to perform a search. You can employ several methods to look up friends. For starters, you can use the **Search** box at the top of any Facebook page. Start typing in a name and Facebook immediately tries to display a list of possible matches, as shown in Figure 6.1. For a complete listing to peruse, click **See More Results** at the bottom of the menu. This opens a search results page similar to Figure 6.2; click the **People** filter link in the left column to view people rather than all the other types of pages.

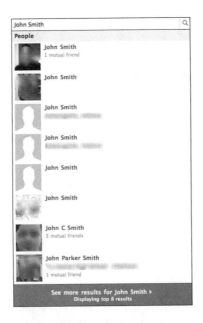

FIGURE 6.1   You can use the Search box to look for a specific person on Facebook.

FIGURE 6.2   Scroll through the results page to find the person you're looking for.

As you can see on the results page, you can use the tools to send a friend request or a message. For example, you might need to message someone to verify it's who you think it is. To view a person's profile page, click his name link. Depending on his privacy setting, you might not be able to view much of his profile. To befriend him, click the **Add Friend** button. He will have to confirm your request before he is added to your Facebook friend list.

Another way to search for friends is to look through the recommendations and common friendships through existing friends. You can do this in several ways. If you click the **Find Friends** link on the Home page (over on the left side of the page under the Favorites category) or the **Find Friends** button on the navigation bar, Facebook displays the Friends app, as shown in Figure 6.3. The top of the page lists recommendations from others and pending friend requests. Another part of the page offers to help you find friends through your email contacts lists from services such as Yahoo! or Windows Live. In other words, Facebook checks your email address book against users' email addresses on the site and tells you about any matches. You'll have to okay access to your email client to perform this task.

The lower portion of the page, shown in Figure 6.4, lists people you might know. If you've already added some friends, this section lists suggestions based on people you've already added to your list. These are typically friends of friends. As a new user, you won't see friend suggestions until you start adding friends. If you do see some listed, you can click the **Add Friend** button to invite them to be your friend.

NOTE: To search through your contacts or address book, you must give Facebook the password for the email account. If you're not comfortable doing this, you might want to forgo this search method entirely. To learn more about Facebook's privacy and security settings, see Lesson 7, "Guarding Your Privacy."

FIGURE 6.3 Use the Friends page to locate friends on Facebook or through your email account.

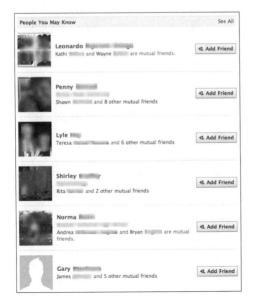

FIGURE 6.4 You can also find friends by looking through Facebook suggestions based on the friends of friends.

TIP: When you add a new friend, you can use Facebook's friend sug-
gestion feature to connect the person to other friends you both
know. This feature is especially helpful if your friend is new to
Facebook. Open the person's profile page, click his or her **Friends**
link, and look for an option for selecting friends to suggest and
send along to the people you think might be interested in knowing
the new friend.

Responding to Friends Who Find You

While you're busy inviting people to be your friends, don't forget to look
for friend requests from other people. When you're the lucky recipient of
an invitation from another Facebook user, it appears on your Home page
as a friend request next to the Find Friends link on the left side, or as a red
number up among the three notifications icons on the blue navigation bar.
Depending on your notifications settings, Facebook might also alert you
with an email if you've turned on the requests feature. When you do find
yourself with a friend request, such as the one shown in Figure 6.5, simply
click the **Confirm** button to add the person to your friends list.

If you're having trouble remembering who the person is or how you're
acquainted, you can click the person's picture to view his or her profile
first, and then decide to add that person as a friend or not. You can also
click the **Mutual Friends** link to learn which mutual friends you have in
common. If you're still having trouble figuring out who the person is, you
can click the **Not Now** button to hide the request and deal with it another
time. To revisit hidden requests, select **See Hidden Requests**.

If you delete a friend request, the person who sent it never knows.
However, they may send you another request in the future.

FIGURE 6.5   Remember to check your notifications for requests and invitations.

Viewing and Editing Friends

After you start accumulating friends on Facebook, you'll want to view their profiles from time to time and see what they're up to online, or check out their latest photo or video postings. For starters, when you open your profile page, Facebook displays a random list of friends in a Friends box, as shown in Figure 6.6.

You can click a friend to view his or her profile. You can also click on a friend listed on the Home page in the news feed, or you can click on a friend listed on your timeline postings. You can also open your entire Friends list and access profiles from there, too.

Viewing Friends

To see everyone on your Friends list, click the **See All** link found in the Friends box area on your profile page. This opens a page similar to the one shown in Figure 6.7. If you're using a Mac or another web browser, a dialog box might open instead.

FIGURE 6.6   You can view your friends in the timeline's Friends box.

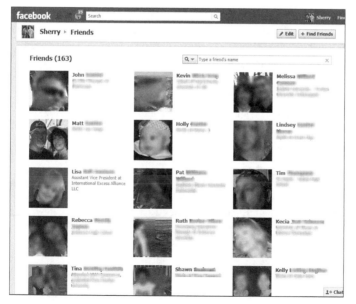

FIGURE 6.7   The Friends list is simply a listing of all your Facebook friends.

To view any friend's profile in the list, just click the person's name or photo.

Organizing Friends into Lists

If you like organization, you'll love Facebook's various Friends lists. You can group your friends into lists, which is particularly useful if you have hundreds of them on Facebook. For example, you may have a list for family and another for close friends, and still another list filled with casual acquaintances. Lists can help you keep track of different groups at different times, or send out messages to everyone in a group all at once.

If you're like most people, you probably talk about some subjects with everybody and other subjects with only those who are close to you. For example, you may freely express your political or religious views, but not everyone on your Friends list or network may want to share in those views. So, you end up having private conversations with some, and more public conversations with others. You can make sure your separate worlds don't collide on Facebook using Friends lists as a tool for communicating and organizing.

Facebook starts you out with three default lists: Close Friends, Acquaintances, and Restricted. These lists are empty until you add people to them. Facebook also creates *smart lists* that automatically update themselves based on profile info, such as relatives you befriend on Facebook. You can also create your own unique lists. When you create a customized list, you can use it to view only news stories from people on that list. You can also selectively post a status update viewable only by the people on that list. You can summon a customized list at any time by clicking the audience selector and selecting the list name.

To create a customized Friends list, follow these steps:

1. Display your Home page and look for the Lists category (see Figure 6.8) in the left pane area; click **Lists**. (Note: If the category is not displayed, click **More** to unhide it.) Facebook opens the Lists page, as shown in Figure 6.9.

2. Click the **Create a List** button at the top of the page.

FIGURE 6.8   Locate the Lists category.

FIGURE 6.9   The Lists page.

3. In the Create a List dialog box that appears (see Figure 6.10), type a name for the new list in the List Name field and click **Create List**.

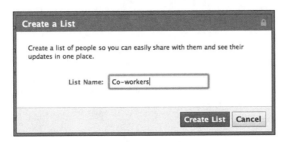

FIGURE 6.10   Give your new list a name.

Facebook opens the new list's page, as shown in Figure 6.11.

FIGURE 6.11   The new list's page appears; click the Add Friends link to start filling it with people.

4. Click the **Add Friends** link. Facebook opens the list, as shown in Figure 6.12.

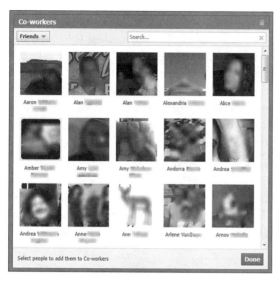

FIGURE 6.12   Facebook lets you add or remove people in a list.

5. You can scroll through and click on people you want to add to the new list, or you can type their names in the Search field.

6. When you finish adding friends to the list, click **Done**.

After you create a new list, Facebook saves it and displays it under the Lists category on the Home page. If you click the list name, the news feed view switches to show only stories from the people on the list. To view the list itself, just click the **Manage List** button in the top-right corner, and then click **Add/Remove Friends**. This opens the same box you used to add friends. You can add more, or deselect the ones you want to remove from the list as needed.

Your customized list is just for you; no one else can see your lists.

To remove a list entirely, display the list's news feed view, click **Manage List**, and click the **Delete List** button; then click **Delete List**.

Unfriending Friends

As your Friends list grows, you may encounter an occasion in which you want to "unfriend" someone. For example, if the person turns out to be a notorious spammer or you have a falling out of some kind, you can remove the person from your list, or perhaps you want to pare down your list to just people you actually know in some way. There's no official declaration of this action; however, if your friend goes looking for you in her Friends list, your name won't appear anymore.

To remove a friend from your list, display his or her profile page and click the **Report/Block** link, or click the cog-like icon in the top-right corner and choose **Report/Block**. A dialog box of options appears, as shown in Figure 6.13. Click the **Unfriend** option and click **Continue**. A confirmation box appears announcing you are no longer friends; click **Okay**.

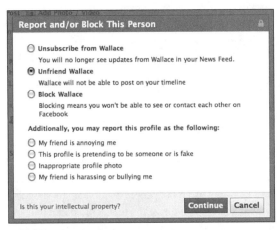

FIGURE 6.13   A friend removal action is permanent.

There's no undo button for a friend removal. If you do want to "re-friend" them again at a later time, you'll have to beg them to be your friend again through a friend request.

When you remove a friend, they can no longer post on your timeline. If you're looking for a more serious solution, you might want to block them instead. This prevents you both from contacting each other again.

Another option is just to unsubscribe. As you can see in Figure 6.13, you can unsubscribe from their posts, which means you're still Facebook

friends, but you won't see their stories anymore out on the Home page
news feed.

TIP: What about when someone unfriends you for no good reason?
When you discover you've been unfriended, try not to take it per-
sonally. Sooner or later you're bound to encounter someone in your
group who gets angry and goes on a tirade unfriending people, like
a relative on the warpath or a vengeful coworker. It might even happen by accident. Just shake it off and keep enjoying the more "sta-
ble" friends you have left.

CAUTION: In addition to removing a friend, you can also use the
reporting tools in the Report and/or Block This Person box to
report harassment, bullying, or inappropriate content. Facebook
takes this very seriously, so pursue these options only as a last
resort.

Subscribing to People

When you add friends on Facebook, you're automatically subscribing to
their posts. New to Facebook, you can also subscribe to people you're not
necessarily friends with but want to keep track of, such as celebrities or
political figures. Called *subscriptions* in Facebook, you can view their public
updates as part of your news feed stories on the Home page. To turn on the
subscription feature, visit the person's page and click the **Subscribe** button.

When you subscribe, you can control what types of updates you view as
well as types of content, such as life events or photos. Simply move the
mouse pointer over the person's **Subscribed** button to display a menu of
viewing options. You'll also find an **Unsubscribe** option in case you ever
want to stop viewing the person's postings.

NOTE: If you don't see a **Subscribe** button, that particular person
doesn't allow subscribing.

To view a list of people you're subscribing to, display your timeline page
and look for the Subscriptions box. If the box is not in view below the
cover photo, click the **More** arrow next to the boxes for Friends, Photos,
Map, and Likes. When you click the arrow, other boxes come into view,

including the Subscriptions box. Click the **Subscriptions** link to open the Subscriptions page, shown in Figure 6.14, listing people you've subscribed to and the number of friend subscriptions you currently have. You can use this page to control what types of information individual subscriptions post on your news feed.

If you allow it, others who are not your friends can subscribe to you as well. This feature is not turned on by default. To activate your own subscription feature, follow this link: www.facebook.com/about/subscribe. Open the description page about the feature and click the **Allow Subscribers** button.

FIGURE 6.14   Use the Subscriptions page to manage the people you subscribe to.

Summary

In this lesson, you learned how to look for friends on Facebook and respond to friend requests. You also learned how to view your Friends list and organize your friends into customized lists. Finally, you learned how to "unfriend" a friend and subscribe to others. In the next lesson, you learn how to use Facebook's privacy controls.

LESSON 7
Guarding Your Privacy

In this lesson, you learn how to protect yourself on Facebook by logging in more smartly, changing your privacy settings, and blocking apps and people as needed.

Understanding Privacy and Security Settings on Facebook

Privacy and security are the number-one concerns on the Internet, and are particularly relevant in the world of social networking. Identity theft is a daily threat, and spammers lurk behind many websites, trying to nab your email address. Guarding yourself online is more important than ever. Along with these dangers, a social networking site such as Facebook also throws in the risks of humiliation, embarrassment, and criticism if you end up posting information you're not supposed to or revealing far too much information to the wrong people. So, how do you begin to protect yourself and still network freely?

The reality is anything you post on Facebook has the potential to be publicly available. This includes your picture and your profile information, such as political views, relationship status, and so on. Facebook does do all it can to protect your personal information, but things happen, hackers can attack, and so on. You may think that only people you allow to be your friends on Facebook can view your info, but that's not the case. There are ways of finding someone's profile on Facebook. Potential employers, law enforcement, teachers, and anyone else determined to do so can find a way to see your profile. If your privacy settings are lax, even a simple search engine can access your profile.

Companies and third-party developers that partner with Facebook can also access your information when allowed. Per Facebook's policy, advertisers who sell products on Facebook can access your information, so safeguarding the info is also up to those companies. Hundreds of third-party applications are available on Facebook, and to make use of them, you must allow them access to your information. In doing so, the potential exists for unscrupulous third-party developers to misuse your data. Because you've allowed them access to the info by adding the application to your account, Facebook can't do much about it.

The bottom line is that taking steps to protect yourself is up to you. Thankfully, you can pursue some strategies to help battle privacy and security breaches, or even stop them from occurring.

Pursuing Protection Strategies

Despite the possibilities for exposure and risk, don't let the fear of privacy and security keep you from enjoying your Facebook experience. You can keep yourself relatively safe just by following a few simple practices:

▶ First and foremost, use common sense when participating in any online endeavor. If something seems risky, it probably is. If someone from your Facebook network emails you about a get-rich plan, you can be sure it's a scam, so don't take the bait.

▶ Never give out personal or sensitive information in a public forum. For example, don't post your cell phone number so that it can be read in everyone's Facebook news feed. You're just asking for trouble.

▶ If Facebook users stalk you or harass you, block their access to your profile and report them to Facebook.

▶ Although the profile information form (see Lesson 2, "Setting Up a Facebook Account") has places for it, you're not required to place personal information of any kind in your profile. For example, if you don't feel comfortable adding your home or work address and phone numbers, don't do it. You can share this type of information through a private email on a "need-to-know" basis.

▶ If you're worried about spammers, consider using a free email address from a site such as Google or Yahoo! for your Facebook account. This can help you protect your main email address from unwanted exposure.

▶ Always be leery of links to sites outside of Facebook that come to you via friends. Make sure the site is legitimate before giving out information. Phishing, the practice of tricking people into revealing sensitive data, is widespread, but you can usually spot these threats by their poor grammar and typos, so keep your eyes peeled.

▶ Even though Facebook advocates honesty, people aren't always what or who they seem to be online. Be skeptical, cautious, and vigilant when it comes to meeting new people online.

▶ When it comes to deciding whether to post something, just ask yourself whether your mom or your employer would be comfortable with it. For example, do you really want your mom or your boss to see a picture of you at that wild party last weekend? Better to err on the side of good judgment with regard to your personal information and pictures.

▶ Finally, make use of the controls Facebook offers to help you stay safe on the site. Why let useful privacy control settings go to waste?

The rest of this lesson shows practical steps you can take to protect your privacy and security on Facebook, which has revamped a lot of the security settings recently. Even if you're already familiar with Facebook, you might want to peruse what's changed to make sure that you're well protected and current.

> CAUTION: Be sure to safeguard other people's info on Facebook, too. For example, refrain from forwarding email messages with the original senders' addresses left in them.

Controlling Account Access

One of the best ways to control your Facebook account is to use some smart login practices. When you log in to your account from the top of the main Facebook page, shown in Figure 7.1, you have the option of checking the **Keep me logged in** check box. This feature tells Facebook to keep you logged in until you decide to log out. Although this might seem like a handy way to avoid typing in your ID and password each time you access your account, it's actually a problem if you're using Facebook on a shared computer. For example, if you're using a computer at a public library, school, or workplace, other users access the computer after you. If you forget to log out, the next user at the computer can access your account. In other words, you've left the door to your information wide open.

FIGURE 7.1   Facebook's login page has a check box to keep yourself signed in if you want.

TIP: Worried about a breach with your Facebook account? You can reset your Facebook password with just a few quick clicks. Good passwords always include a combination of letters, numbers, and symbols (if allowed). To reset a password, click the drop-down arrow in the navigation bar (the downward-pointing arrow icon next to the Home link) and click **Account Settings** to open the Account Settings page. Click the **Edit** link next to the Password option. Type your current password, type a new password, and retype the new password to confirm it. Click the **Save Changes** button to finish the procedure.

If you use Facebook only from a home computer, the option can be a time-saver. However, if your entire family uses the same computer, they can easily access your account and pose as you online—not that anything bad can come from that, right? Aside from the sarcasm, an unprotected home computer is also vulnerable to people who come in and out of your house, such as babysitters, repairmen, and friends.

To prevent unwanted access entirely, make sure the **Keep me logged in** check box is deselected when you log in to your account. Second, always log out of the site when you've finished by clicking the **Account** drop-down arrow on the navigation bar at the top of any Facebook page and then clicking the **Log Out** option. Do not just click the browser's **Close** button—you must genuinely log out to end the Facebook connection.

Customizing Your Privacy Settings

You can control your privacy on Facebook in several ways. Just about all the privacy settings let you specify whether you want to post the information for all to see, share it just among your friends, or customize it so only selected friend lists or individuals see it. Although the Facebook designers keep tweaking the controls, which may result in different screens than those shown here, the basic premise is still the same—these settings enable users to choose exactly how they want their information made available to others.

Log in to Facebook and click the **Account** menu drop-down arrow at the top of any Facebook page, and then click the **Privacy Settings** option from the pop-up menu that appears (see Figure 7.2).

FIGURE 7.2   Access privacy settings through the Account menu.

Facebook displays the Privacy Settings page, similar to Figure 7.3. The page features links for controlling how you connect with people, how tags are applied, how applications and websites interact with your info, how others view your old posts, and how to make a block list for blocking unwanted users and apps.

FIGURE 7.3   The Privacy Settings page is the place to go to set privacy controls.

The first thing to set is a default privacy setting, which applies to any postings that don't already have their own individual privacy controls. For example, if you use a Facebook app to post items from your Blackberry device, the default privacy setting you specify dictates how the information is shared on Facebook. You can choose **Public**, **Friends**, or **Custom**. Most users are happy with the **Friends** setting.

If you scroll down the page a bit, you'll find the rest of the privacy settings, as shown in Figure 7.4. You'll learn more about these settings in the remainder of this lesson.

Controlling How You Connect

Use the How You Connect settings to control who can look up your profile page information (also known as the timeline), send you friend requests and messages, post on your timeline, and view other timeline posts. When you click the **Edit Settings** link next to the How You Connect category (refer to Figure 7.4), Facebook opens the How You Connect box, as shown in Figure 7.5.

FIGURE 7.4   Scroll down the Privacy Settings page to see more features.

FIGURE 7.5   Use these settings to control how people interact with you on Facebook.

Off to the right side of each setting is an "audience selector," which is basically a drop-down menu (Figure 7.5 shows one displayed) that lets you choose who is allowed to interact with you. Simply click the selector and click an option. Depending on the privacy setting, the options may include all or several of the following:

▶ **Everyone**—The most open level of privacy, allowing anyone on Facebook to view the information.

▶ **Friends of Friends**—Only immediate friends and friends of friends can view the information.

▶ **Friends**—Only people you've friended on Facebook can view the information.

▶ **Only Me**—You're the only one who can use the feature.

▶ **Custom**—Enables you to customize exactly which friends can or cannot view the information.

If you have created lists of people on Facebook, such as grouping all your family members into a list, the lists may also appear as an option for selection.

After you've made your selection(s), click the **Done** button to return to the Privacy Settings page.

> TIP: If you're worried about people seeing your picture on your Facebook profile, consider using an image other than an actual photo of you. For example, you might use a picture related to your hobbies or interests instead. Visit Lesson 2 to learn more about adding and changing a profile picture.

Controlling How Tags Work

Facebook tags are used to link a person, page, or place to a status update, photo, or video. Basically, a tag is an identifier. Anytime you tag a person, Facebook lets her know about it, and the posted item is visible to everyone in that person's timeline. For example, let's say you went to a birthday party and took some photos of the guest of honor and the other partygoers. You can add a tag to the photo on Facebook that lets your friend know she's in the photo and helps other friends know about the photo, too.

New to Facebook, the How Tags Work privacy category gives you more control regarding how tags are handled. You can review tags before they're posted to your or your friend's timelines, control who is allowed to see the tags after they appear in your timeline, identify potential photos of you for tagging, and let friends tag you in places you visit. To view the tag settings, click the **Edit Settings** link next to the How Tags Work category on the Privacy Settings page (refer to Figure 7.4). Facebook opens the How Tags Work box, as shown in Figure 7.6. You can use this box to turn features on or off or specify who views your tags.

FIGURE 7.6   Use these settings to control how tags behave.

After you finish setting tag options, click **Done** to return to the Privacy Settings page.

Controlling Apps and Websites

Applications and games are add-on programs that work with Facebook. They come in a wide variety of types and functions, from the serious to the silly. Some applications, or *apps* for short, are part of your Facebook account by default, such as the Notes and Photos applications. We cover applications in greater detail in Lesson 13, "Adding Applications," but as they relate to privacy, let's talk about how to control them a bit here so you're better informed when more apps start crossing your path later.

Here's a fact: Most of the applications and games you add in Facebook access your profile information. You typically can't use an application unless you allow this. Sounds logical, yes? But did you know that applications your friends allow access to can also access information about you just because you're their friend? Sneaky, eh? You can de-authorize this access using the Apps, Games and Websites page as part of the Facebook privacy settings. You can also control what types of information are shared. To find your way to application privacy settings, click the **Edit Settings** link located next to the heading Apps and Websites on the Privacy Settings page (refer to Figure 7.4). The Apps, Games and Websites page, shown in Figure 7.7, offers several options:

> ▶ **Apps you use**—Lists recent applications, games, and websites you're using with Facebook. You can remove apps or turn them

off using the options listed here, or click the Edit Settings button
to view a complete list.

FIGURE 7.7   The Apps, Games and Websites page lets you control what
information applications and partner websites can access.

▶ **How people bring your info to apps they use**—Control what
information is shared from your profile when your friends use
Facebook-enhanced applications and related websites.

▶ **Instant personalization**—Turn on or off personalization shared
with Facebook's partner sites, such as Docs.com or Yelp, when
your friends use them.

▶ **Public search**—Enable or disable public search controls regarding your timeline. Although technically this isn't related to apps
and games, it is sort of related to website searches, so the option
appears on this page.

To control individual applications themselves, you must visit the App
Settings page, shown in Figure 7.8. To find your way to this page, click
the Edit Settings button next to the Apps You Use category (refer to
Figure 7.7).

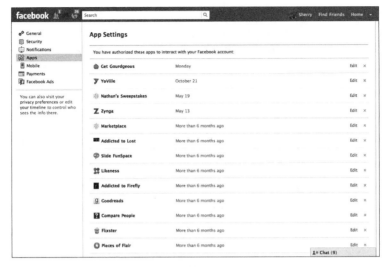

FIGURE 7.8   The App Settings page keeps a running list of your Facebook applications.

From the list of applications, you can edit the settings of each application, read more about the application itself, or remove it entirely:

▶ Click the **Edit** link to display more information about the app or fine-tune how it works with your information.

▶ To remove an application entirely, click the **X** button at the far-right end of the application listing and click **Remove**. You'll be prompted when the process is over; click **Okay**.

To learn more about applications and how they work in Facebook, see Lesson 13.

Limiting Past Posts

Another new option to the privacy settings is the ability to limit who sees your older posts. As you've already learned in Lesson 4, "Navigating Your Timeline," you can quickly change the audience for any particular post on your timeline using the inline controls, but what if you want to reset all of your past postings at once? Ideally, the Limit Past Posts feature on the Privacy Settings page is handy if you've previously had all your postings set to Public, which means everyone can see them, and you want to reset all the past postings to be viewed only by your friends. Keep in mind that if you enact this tool, you can't undo it. Anyone who added comments to the older postings will lose access to those comments. To activate the feature, click the **Manage Past Post Visibility** link next to the Limit the Audience for Past Posts category found on the Privacy Settings page. This opens a dialog box, shown in Figure 7.9. Click the Limit Old Posts button to start the procedure.

FIGURE 7.9   Old posts too public? No problem; limit them retroactively using this privacy setting tool.

Blocking People and Apps

The final option to cover under Facebook's privacy controls is how to block other Facebook members and apps.

This particular feature is used to restrict someone from bothering you or accessing you on Facebook. When you block users, they can no longer see your profile information or interact with you through Facebook features. This also means you can no longer see them on Facebook. Blocking them only knocks them out of contacting you in Facebook. Outside of Facebook is another matter.

From the Privacy Settings page (refer to Figure 7.4), click the **Manage Blocking** link next to the Blocked People and Apps category. This opens the Manage Blocking page, as shown in Figure 7.10.

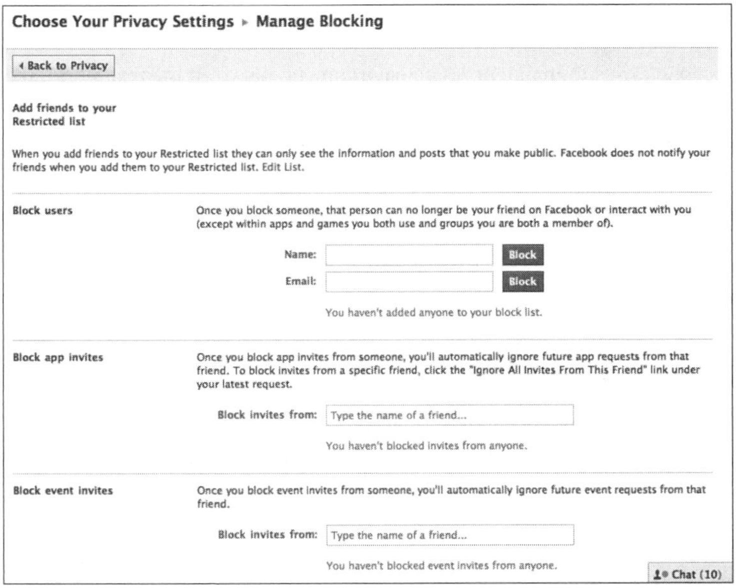

FIGURE 7.10 Use the Block users area to block other Facebook members.

To block someone, just type his or her name in the Name box and press **Enter** (**Return**) or click the **Block** button. This opens the Block People dialog box. Simply identify the correct person you're blocking, click the **Block** button next to their name, and the deed is done. The blocked user's name is added to the Restricted list. You can add more people to the list, or even block them based on their email address instead.

You can also use the Manage Blocking page to block application invites. For example, if your friend is constantly inviting you to play *FarmVille* or *Mafia Wars*, you can stop all the application invites from that friend, including *FarmVille* and whatever other apps the friend is freely sharing with you. Just type your friend's name in the **Block invites from** field located under the Block app invites area of the page.

If you're tired of responding to certain event invitations, you can block them as well. Under the Block event invites area of the page, you can type the friend's name and turn off future event invitations from him.

Reporting Abuse

Facebook tries to maintain a safe environment, but as in the real world, the online world is often fraught with illegal, offensive, and inappropriate material and conduct. Nudity, pornography, harassment, hate speech, and unwelcome contact are against Facebook's rules. If you spot something along these lines, you can report it to Facebook. To contact them directly, you can email abuse@facebook.com, and they'll look in to the problem. In addition to this route, you can find Report links scattered throughout the Facebook pages. You can click a link to report a problem. For example, if you encounter a pornographic picture in someone's photo album, you can click the **Report This Photo** link.

You can check out Facebook's Security page for more help with questionable material and conduct and how to find help. To access the page, click the **Help** link at the bottom of any Facebook page to open the Help Center, and then click the **Report Abuse or Policy Violations** link to view related links. You can also click the **Account** menu drop-down arrow at the top of the Facebook page and click **Help** to find your way to the security info.

> TIP: Anytime you want to refresh your knowledge of Facebook's terms of service, click the **Terms** link at the bottom of any Facebook page. This opens a page with information, links to privacy settings, and so on.

Summary

In this lesson, you learned all about Facebook's privacy settings and how to keep your data safe while using the website. In the next lesson, you learn more about communicating through Facebook.

LESSON 8

Communicating Through Facebook

In this lesson, you learn how to use Facebook tools to communicate with your friends, coworkers, family, and so on. You'll learn how to send private messages using the Facebook inbox, share links and notes, and chat live.

How to Communicate on Facebook

You can't have a social networking site without avenues to communicate, and Facebook has plenty. You've already learned how to express yourself on your timeline page by posting a story. This particular form of communication is generated by you for the purpose of letting people know what you're up to. When they pop by your page, they see your activities and any status updates you posted. They can also see your stories out on the Home page in the news feed scroll.

Communicating by posts goes both ways—friends can write on your page, and you can also write on your friends' pages to communicate with them. You might write a new posting, or comment on existing postings on a friend's timeline. Anyone else who views the friend's page can also see your postings and comments (unless your friend has restricted viewing).

If you join a group, you can communicate through postings on the group page. You can learn more about Facebook groups in Lesson 11, "Joining Groups." As with any other posting task on Facebook, when you share postings in a group, everyone in the group can see them.

If you're looking for more direct, less-public ways to communicate, you can use the Facebook Messages feature to send and receive messages. Just as with any email client you use, the Messages feature has options for reading messages, creating and sending messages, and organizing received messages. If you're looking for more immediate communication, try Facebook's live chat feature. You can talk with your friends (via your keyboard) who are logged in at the same time as you.

Sending and Receiving Messages

You can send and receive messages through the Facebook Messages page. It works just like an email client, letting you send personal messages to your Facebook friends using a central page that acts like an inbox. You don't have to know the person's email address to send him a message; you just need to know his name. You can also attach items to a message, such as a photo or link.

The Messages page also keeps track of your chat conversations. They're saved along with Facebook email messages and listed on the page as well until you delete them.

To view the Messages page, click the **Messages** link under the Favorites heading on the left side of the Home page. Figure 8.1 shows an example of a typical Messages page.

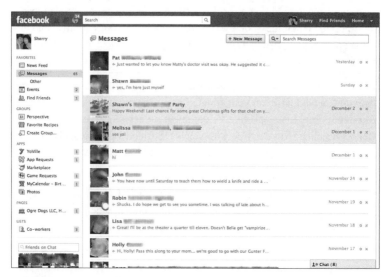

FIGURE 8.1   Use the Messages page to send personal messages to your Facebook friends.

TIP: Facebook lets you know how many messages you have waiting in the inbox by displaying the number next to the Messages link on the Home page or on the Email notifications icon up in the navigation bar.

When you click the **Messages** category, a list of all the messages you've received appears, with the most recent messages at the top of the list. Messages include the sender's picture, if applicable, and the first line of the message text. Facebook also includes the date of the message. To read a message, click it to open the full message page, similar to Figure 8.2. You can click the message content line to open the message. After it's opened, you can write a reply to the message, attach other items to the reply, and send it back to the person.

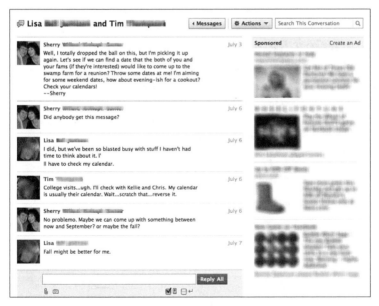

FIGURE 8.2   When you open a message to read it, a new page opens, along with a Reply text box you can use to send back a reply.

To reply to a message you've received, click in the **Reply** text box at the bottom of the message and type out your reply, and then click the **Reply** button (unless the message is directed to more than one person, then click **Reply All**).

If you're messaging one person and keep replying to the original message, the message text accumulates similar to a thread on a news posting or discussion board, as shown in Figure 8.2. You can see the previous messages along with a Reply box for continuing the conversation. To return to the Messages page, click the **Messages** button at the top.

CAUTION: Be careful about replying to messages that were addressed to multiple people. Because they were sent out to a bunch of people, the reply goes to the entire group, too.

Managing Messages

You can use the message indicator icons located on the far-right side of your messages to see the status of each message in your inbox. You can click the circle icon to change the message status to Unread (solid dot) or Read (hollow dot). One way to tell read messages from unread messages is by their background shading. Unread messages appear with a light blue shading as their background color. Read messages have no shading.

Here's how you can manage your messages:

▶ To mark a message as unread, click the hollow circle next to the message.

▶ To mark a message as read again without opening the message, click the blue circle icon next to the message.

▶ You can archive messages you no longer want to view. Click the X button next to the message.

▶ To search through your messages, click inside the **Search Messages** field in the top-right corner and type a word or phrase you want to search for, and then press **Enter** or **Return**.

You can also manage individual messages by opening the message in its own page. Click the **Actions** button at the top of the page to view a menu of options, as shown in Figure 8.3. You can mark the message as unread, forward it to another friend, move it to the Other folder (a default folder for mailing lists and emails from people who aren't Facebook friends), archive it, report it, or open it in a chat window.

FIGURE 8.3   Use the Actions menu to manage individual messages.

To permanently remove any message instead of just archiving it, you can click the **Delete Messages** option. You can then choose which messages to delete in the conversation (if it's more than one) by clicking the check boxes in front of the text, and then clicking the **Delete All** button.

Sending a Message

You can send messages to other Facebook users, or to people you know outside of the Facebook environment, as long as you know their email addresses. To send a message on Facebook, display the Messages page and follow these steps:

1. Click the **New Message** button. Facebook opens the New Message form box, as shown in Figure 8.4.

2. In the New Message form, click in the **To** field and type in the name, friend list (if you want to email a group of friends on Facebook), or email address. As you start typing, Facebook displays a list of possible matches to choose from; you can select a name from the list or keep typing.

To remove a name that's added to the To field, just click its **X** button, or select the name and press **Delete**.

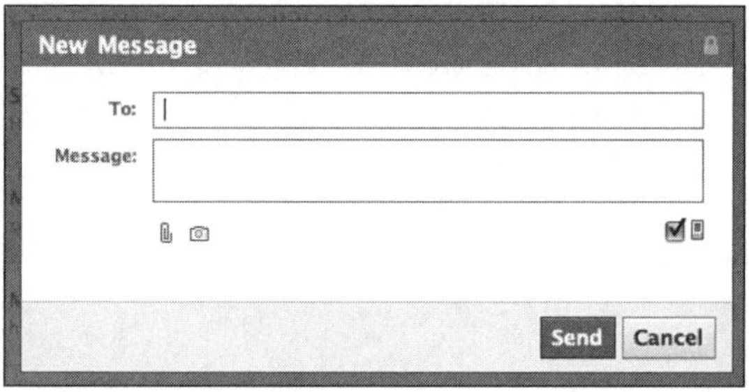

FIGURE 8.4   The New Message form.

3. Click in the **Message** box and type in your message text.

   Optionally, you can use the buttons below the Message box to attach a file or photo, or send the message to a mobile phone (if the person uses a mobile device to receive Facebook messages).

4. When you're ready to send, click the **Send** button.

You can send a message to more than one person—just add additional names to the To field. You can add up to 20 names per message, according to the latest info in the Facebook Help Center at the time of writing.

Sharing Links

You can share web content you stumble across on the Internet with your friends on Facebook. For example, if you find a YouTube clip you want others to see, or if you read an interesting news article you want others to read, you can share a link to the material. You can add links directly into the status update box, as shown in Figure 8.5.

Click in the field and type the URL to which you want to link. You can also paste a link you've copied from your browser window. Facebook Publisher automatically creates a story that includes a thumbnail of the page and any associated information. When you click **Post**, Facebook adds the link to the story. In Figure 8.6, a video link appears with the story in the news feed.

FIGURE 8.5   Use the status update box to add a comment and a link.

FIGURE 8.6   After you add the link, it appears on your page and in the news feed.

If you want to link to a particular item in the news feed on the Home page, you can quickly share it with others by clicking the **Share** link conveniently located below the posting, such as a photo or a link. When activated, this feature opens a Share box, similar to that shown in Figure 8.7, or a Send as Message box, and you can choose to post the story on your timeline page or send it privately as a message to a friend. Just fill in any details, if needed, and share the item.

FIGURE 8.7   You can share a link to another Facebook posting on your timeline page or as a message to a friend.

NOTE: Facebook's Links app used to be more prominent, but it's still there. You can use the Links page to view a news feed of links you and your friends have posted. To find the app, click the **More** link next to the Apps category on the Home page. Scroll down and click the **Links** link to view a page of link stories.

Blogging with Notes

The Notes feature is another of Facebook's default applications, but it's no longer as front-and-center as it once was. You'll have to dig a little to find it. Because the Facebook developers increased the character count allowed in the status update box, the Notes app is not as necessary. You used to have to open the Notes app to type in large chunks of text you wanted to post, such as a blog entry, for example.

You can still use Notes when you want to share longer paragraphs of text, resembling a document rather than a lengthy status update. You can even add photos to your notes. Notes are perfect for blogging on Facebook and sharing the blog with your friends. When you post a note, it appears on your profile page and in the news feed. You do have the choice of setting a privacy level for the note. After a note is published, others can add their comments to the note.

To find the Notes tool, click the **More** link next to the Apps category heading on the Home page (hover to the far right of the heading to make the link appear). The Apps page opens. Scroll down the page and click the **Notes** link when you find it. Facebook then opens a Notes page that includes notes your friends have posted. Now you're ready to start your own note:

1. From the Notes page, click the Write a Note button at the top.

Facebook displays the Write a Note page with a blank note form, as shown in Figure 8.8.

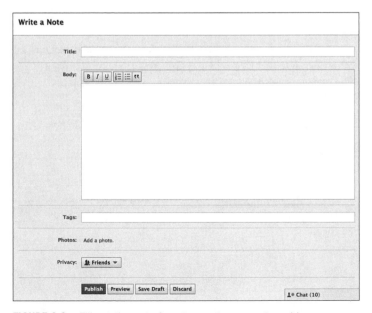

FIGURE 8.8   Fill out the note form to create your note or blog.

2. Click in the **Title** box and type in a title for your note.

3. Click in the **Body** box and type in your note text.

TIP: You can easily copy and paste text from another program into your Facebook Notes feature. For example, you might compose your blog in Microsoft Word and copy the text into the Facebook form.

Optionally, you can tag Facebook friends you mention in your note using the **Tags** field. This lets them know with a notification that they're somehow involved in your note.

Optionally, you can click the **Add a Photo** link (or Choose File in other browsers) to add a photo to the note, or add one from an existing Facebook photo album. When you add a photo, additional options appear for controlling the photo's position on the note page, and a box for adding a caption.

4. Click the **Privacy** drop-down menu and choose an audience level for the note.

5. To preview the note first, click the **Preview** button and check out how your note will look on Facebook. You can publish it from the preview page or click **Edit** to return to the Notes page.

If you prefer to save the draft and open it again later, click the **Save Draft** button. To change your mind about the whole note idea entirely, click the **Discard** button.

6. To publish the note, click the **Publish** button.

Facebook adds the note to your timeline and it also appears in the news feed on the Home page, unless you chose to share it only with a customized friends list.

Chatting with Friends

If messages, notes, and digital pokes aren't enough ways to communicate on Facebook, you can also talk directly to friends using the Chat tool. If a friend is logged on at the same time as you, you can have real-time conversations. If you've chatted with other Chat programs, such as Yahoo! Messenger, you'll find that the Facebook Chat tool works the same way. You can even invite more than one person to chat in the same conversation window.

The first thing to do is check your online status. Look for the Chat bar at the bottom of the browser window. If you're already "online" for chatting, the bar just says Chat. If you're offline, or unavailable for chatting, the bar says Chat (Offline). To toggle your offline status on again, click the **Chat** bar, click the **Options** button, and then click the **Available to Chat** option to unselect it. You can toggle this command on and off. When it's on, a green dot appears on the Chat bar. If it's off, the dot changes to gray. After your status is green, you're good to go.

Now you have to find someone to chat with. Click the **Chat** bar again to see a list of your Facebook friends who are currently online, as shown in Figure 8.9. (You can also see who else is online by viewing the Friends Online list located on the left pane of the Home page.) If they're available for a chat, you'll see them listed in the Chat menu. To start chatting, click the friend's name in the list. Facebook opens a mini chat window, similar to Figure 8.10. Type in what you want to say in the field at the bottom of the chat window, and press **Enter** or **Return**. The text appears in the conversational area of the window, and continues to scroll by as you keep chatting. You can use the scrollbar to revisit parts of the conversation.

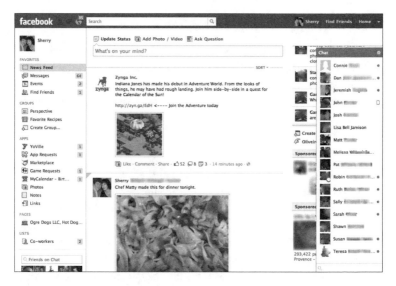

FIGURE 8.9   You can click the Chat bar to view a list of everyone online and see who's available for a chat.

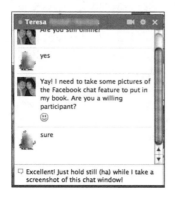

FIGURE 8.10   You can type in the bottom area of the chat window to start chatting.

To close the window and stop chatting, just click the window's **Close** button (**X**) in the upper-right corner. You can also minimize the window to move it out of the way. If the window is minimized, Facebook displays a red balloon icon to let you know the other person has typed in more conversation.

To create a larger chat window, click the **Options** button on the Chat bar, as shown in Figure 8.11, and choose **See Full Conversation**. This takes you to Facebook's Message page, the same one you use to read and send email messages, and displays your chat conversation. To return to the mini-window again, click the **Options** button (it looks like a tiny cog icon) and choose **Open in Chat**.

FIGURE 8.11   Use the Options menu to enhance your chat.

To add another friend to the conversation, click the **Options** button and choose **Add Friends to Chat**. Type in the friend's name in the box at the top of the Chat window and you're ready to keep talking.

Summary

In this lesson, you learned how to communicate with friends on Facebook using messages, notes, links, and chatting. In the next lesson, you'll learn how to share photos.

LESSON 9

Sharing Photos

In this lesson, you learn how to view and add photos in Facebook. You'll learn how to create an album, upload pictures, and publish the whole thing on Facebook. You'll also learn how to tag people in your photos and organize your photos within Facebook.

Sharing Photos on Facebook

Would you believe that Facebook is the largest photo-sharing site on the Web? It's true. It surpasses popular sites such as Photobucket and Flickr, among others. Facebook users upload millions of photos each month. Why? Reasons include because it's easy, a fun way to share stuff about yourself, a perfect way to connect with others, and a great marketing tool, just to list a few. It might also help that Facebook lets you post gobs of photos. As of 2011, users have uploaded more than 100 billion photos on the social networking site. That's a lot of pictures.

Photos you add to Facebook are organized into photo *albums*, just as you would do with printed photographs at home. An album can hold 1 photo or up to 200. You can also create as many albums as you want. You might make an album of vacation pictures, artistic images, snapshots of your friends and family, and so on. When you post photos, you can add captions and tag people in the photos, and other users can add comments to your photos.

All your photo activities on Facebook are handled through a built-in application called, appropriately, Photos. The application, which is part of the default apps available when you start your Facebook account, offers tools for uploading, organizing, and sharing photos.

You can share photos on your profile page (also known as the timeline), in the news feed out on the Home page, in messages and notes, in group postings, and more. One of the easiest ways to view your friends' photos is when you see them posted as a story on the news feed on your Home page, as shown in Figure 9.1. Just click a photo to open the image in its own window, or click the album name located next to the photo to open the associated album.

FIGURE 9.1   Posted photos often appear as stories on the news feed on your Home page.

TIP: If you click the Photos app listed on the Home page, you can open a news feed display showing all the recently posted photos from your Facebook friends. If you don't see the link listed under the Apps heading, click the More link next to the Apps heading and then click Photos.

Another way to view photos is on profile pages. For example, if you're viewing your friend's page, you can click a photo in her timeline, or you can click her **Photos** link and view her listed albums. Figure 9.2 shows an example of photos posted on the timeline of a profile page.

When you select a photo to view, Facebook displays it in the photo viewer window, as shown in Figure 9.3, as a larger image. If there is more than one photo in the album, you can click the navigation arrows on either side of the image to move back and forth between pictures.

FIGURE 9.2 Another way to view photos is on profile pages.

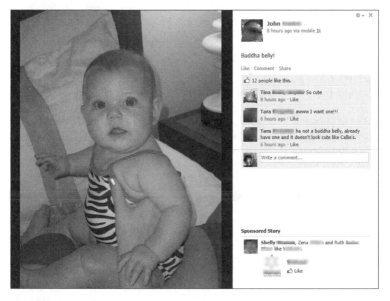

FIGURE 9.3 The Facebook photo viewer lets you see larger versions of your photos.

The viewer window has options for commenting, sharing the photo with others, tagging someone in the photo, or reporting any photo that violates the Facebook terms of service. Not that you need to be reminded, but some restrictions apply as to what types of photos you can share on Facebook. So if you're hoping to start your own online pornography magazine, Facebook is not the way to go. You can check out Facebook's Terms of Service page to learn more about rules and conduct on the site. See Lesson 3, "Finding Help with Facebook Services and Etiquette," to find out more.

NOTE: Tagging is when you identify someone in the photo, and Facebook sends out a notification to the person and mentions it in her timeline. Learn more about tagging later in this lesson.

To add your two cents about the photo, click in the comment box and start typing. Press **Enter** (**Return**) to post the comment. You can also "Like" a photo or share it on your profile page and news feed. Click the **Like** link to add a thumbs-up icon below the photo. Click the **Share** link to open the Share this Photo dialog box where you can share the image on your timeline, in another friend's timeline, in a group, or in a private message.

To exit the window and return to what you were doing on Facebook, just click the **Close** button located in the upper-right corner of the viewer, or press the **Esc** key.

Viewing photos is easy enough, but if you're looking for an all-encompassing spot to view your own photos, visit the Photos page. The next section tells you how.

Viewing the Photos Page

To find your way to the Photos page, click the **Photos** link located at the top of your timeline, underneath your name and cover image. When clicked, the link takes you to the Photos page, as shown in Figure 9.4. The

top section of the page lists all your uploaded albums, including your profile pictures. The bottom portion of the page lists all the photos in which
you've been tagged. You can view a specific photo album, which displays
thumbnails of the images it contains, or you can view full-size individual
pictures just by clicking an image. (You just learned about the photo
viewer in the previous section to see enlarged photos.)

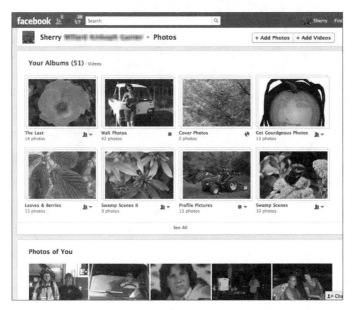

FIGURE 9.4   Use the Photos page to view your photo albums or upload
pictures.

To view an album, click the album name. Take a look at a typical album
page, as shown in Figure 9.5. Here you can view thumbnail images of the
album's content.

As with the individual photos you view with the photo viewer window,
you can also add comments to an album and find options for sharing it
with friends. You might need to scroll down the page a bit to find the links
and comment area. Comments are a great way to converse about the picture, the subject, or the experience it represents. Seeing entire conversations unfold in the comment sections of a single photo or album cover is
not uncommon.

FIGURE 9.5   You can view an album to display thumbnail images of the pictures it contains.

To share an album with another friend, you can click the **Share** link on the album page to open the Share this Album dialog box. From there, you can share the album by posting a link on your timeline or by emailing a link to a friend.

Adding Your Own Photos

Now that you know a little about how to view photos in Facebook, it's time to add some of your own. First, you need to locate and decide which photos you want to share online. After you've figured that out, you're ready to create an album and upload some photos.

> NOTE: You can add a photo in your status update box, too, and post it directly onto your timeline (previously known as the Wall). Just click inside the box, click the **Photo** link (on your profile page) or **Add Photo/Video** link (on the Home page), and then choose an option. You can upload a single photo, grab one from your camera (as long as it's attached to your computer), or start a brand-new album from the status update box.

You can easily create a new photo album from the Photos page. You can also control who has access to your photos using the audience selector control. First, you'll select which photos you want to upload; then you can fill out the album name and description details and post the pictures.

Follow these steps to start an album for the first time:

1. From your profile page, click the **Photos** link to open your Photos page.

2. Click the **Add Photos** button.

3. A standard Select Files or Open Files dialog box appears listing your computer's contents. Navigate to the folder containing the pictures you want to upload and select the files.

   To select multiple photos, you can hold down the **Ctrl** key and click filenames (Mac users can hold down the **Command** key), or if the photos are contiguous, you can hold down the **Shift** key and select the last file in the sequence.

4. Click **Open**. Facebook uploads the files, as shown in Figure 9.6, and you can fill in details about each photo or the album in general.

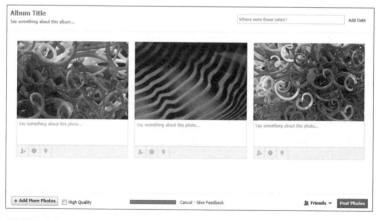

FIGURE 9.6 After you've selected which files to upload, you can specify an album name, location, and audience.

5. To name the album, click the **Album Title** area and type a name for the album.

6. To add a description, click the **Say something about this album** area and type a brief description about the pictures.

7. Optional: In the **Where were these taken** box, type the location in which the pictures were taken and use the Add Date option to add a date, if applicable.

8. Use the **Say something about this photo** area under each picture to add a caption.

9. Click the **Audience Selector** drop-down arrow and select your audience for the album, such as **Public** or **Friends**.

TIP: When you activate the Custom option in the audience selector drop-down menu, a separate dialog box form opens, and you can specify who you want to allow and even who you do not want to allow access to your photos. You can specify people by name, and you can choose to allow an entire customized friend list.

10. When you're done filling out information, click **Post Photos**. Facebook posts the albums on your timeline. To view it at any time, you can open your Photos page and select the album name.

TIP: The album name and other details you enter during the upload process aren't set in stone. You can edit these items at any time, such as changing the audience to just a specific list of friends or changing the album name when you think of something more fitting. To edit album details such as these, see the section "Organizing and Editing Your Photos" later in this lesson.

NOTE: You can invite people outside the Facebook website to view your albums using the public link Facebook provides. Open the album to the Edit Album page and scroll to the bottom to find a unique URL you can copy and paste into an email message. The recipient can then follow the link and view your images. Of course, it would be cooler if they would just join in the fun and make a Facebook account, but that's not required.

NOTE: Back in Lesson 2, "Setting Up a Facebook Account," you learned how to add a profile picture. You can add more profile pictures whenever you want. All your profile pictures are organized in a default album called, appropriately, Profile Pictures. To view this album, just look for it among the other albums on your Photos page. You can edit existing photos, add new ones, and remove ones you no longer want.

Using Other Photo Uploaders

If you're a Mac user, you can add the iPhoto Exporter application to your computer and use it to upload photos from the iPhoto application directly. To find your way to the app, type **Facebook Exporter for iPhoto** into the search box at the top of any Facebook page and press **Enter** (**Return**). Click the **Facebook Exporter for iPhoto** name in the search results listing. Click the **Download App** button and download the Facebook Exporter for iPhoto application. You can then install the application and use iPhoto to upload photos into a Facebook album.

iPhoto Exporter simply adds a Facebook tab to the Export Photos dialog box, as shown in Figure 9.7, where you can create a new album for Facebook or insert the photos in an existing album. You can also use the dialog box to add captions and tags before uploading the images. To navigate to the dialog box and see for yourself, open iPhoto and select the files you want to import. Next, click the **File** menu, and then click **Export**. When the Export Photos dialog box opens, you'll have to log in to your Facebook account to start the process. After your browser logs you in, you're returned to the Export Photos dialog box, where you can continue the process of uploading the files. Just click the **Export** button and follow the prompts. When the import is complete, you can review the album on Facebook and approve the uploaded images. After you've approved the images, you can post the album to your profile, and you're done.

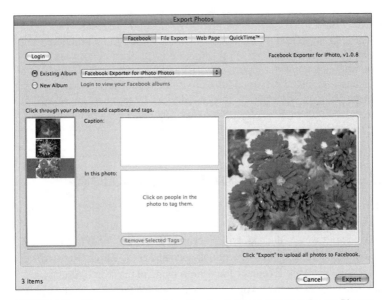

FIGURE 9.7 Mac users can add a Facebook tab to iPhoto's Export Photos dialog box for uploading image files.

If you have photos on a camera phone, you can upload them to Facebook, too. Depending on the type of phone you use, you might need to follow different uploading procedures. For example, you can use your personalized upload email address to upload photos from a feature phone, or if you're using an iPhone, a completely different set of steps is required. Learn more about Facebook's mobile features in Lesson 16, "Making Facebook Mobile."

Tagging Photos

Tagging is a popular activity on Facebook. Tagging is when you identify someone in a story, photo, or video. When you tag people, Facebook lets them know with a notification so they can go take a look at the story. The tag also appears as a story in their mini-feed on their profile page. In the case of photos, you can tag people to identify them in the picture. You can even tag people in a photo who aren't on Facebook and send them an email message.

To tag a person in a picture, follow these steps:

1. Open the photo you want to tag.

2. Click the **Tag This Photo** link.

3. The mouse pointer turns into a cross-hair pointer when you move it over the photo. Click the person or area you want to identify in the photo to open a tag box, as shown in Figure 9.8.

FIGURE 9.8   You can tag people in a photo to identify them.

4. Click a name from the list or type in the person's name.

   If you type someone's name who isn't in your Friends list, you have the option of emailing the person a link to the image, even if they don't have a Facebook account.

5. Click the **Tag** button, and the person is tagged.

6. Click the **Done Tagging** link when you finish tagging everyone in the photo.

When you add a tag, anyone viewing the photo can move his or her mouse over the people in the photo and view the tag that points out who each person is. Very handy, don't you think?

To de-tag a person, you can reopen the photo and click the **Edit** link, then click the **X** button next to the person's name and click the **Save** button to finish the edit. People you've tagged can also remove their tags from your photos using the same step.

You can also tag yourself in someone else's photos, but they'll have to approve of the tag before everyone else can see it.

New to Facebook, you can also tag locations in your photos. Click the **Add Location** link in the photo viewer window and specify a location where the photo was taken. You can type a specific location or choose an existing place, such as a city. Use the **Change Date** link to designate a special date for the photo.

Organizing and Editing Your Photos

Organizing and editing your photos after you have created an album is easy. For example, you might decide you need to reorganize the photos or add captions. Or you might want to delete a photo or completely remove an entire album.

To revisit an album and make changes, click the **Photos** link on your profile page. Locate the album you want to work with, and then click the album name to open the album. Facebook displays all the thumbnail images included in the album, similar to Figure 9.9. You can reorganize your photos in this view. Simply click and drag them around on the album page to reposition their order.

What about adding more photos, you ask? That's easy. If you click the **Add Photos** button in the top-right corner, you can upload more photos.

FIGURE 9.9   To edit an album, start by opening the album's thumbnail view.

NOTE: There are two view modes you can use while displaying your album's thumbnails: Album View and Comment View. Album View shows the pictures horizontally at the top of the page and the comments down below. Comment View displays the pictures vertically, with the comments along the side. You can flip back and forth between views using the buttons up in the top-right corner of the page.

If you want to edit album details, such as the title or individual photos, click the **Edit Album** link (refer to Figure 9.9). This opens the Edit Album page, shown in Figure 9.10. This page displays all the photos, along with options for adding or editing captions, deleting a photo, moving a photo to another album, or designating a new album cover. The album cover is just the photo that appears as the main photo in the listing of albums and when the story is posted on your timeline or news feed. By default, the Photos application makes the first photo the album cover, but you can choose any photo in the album as the cover.

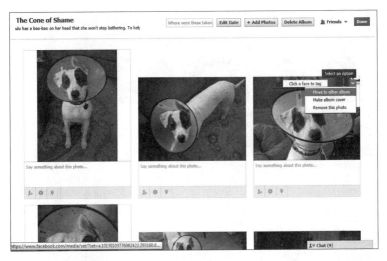

FIGURE 9.10   Open an album's Edit Album page to find options for editing, organizing, and deleting albums.

You have several editing options to choose from, as follows:

▶ To change the album name, description, or location, click the existing text at the top of the page and type in new information.

▶ To change the date for the album, click the **Edit Date** button and choose another.

▶ To add a caption, click in the **Description** box below each photo and type one up.

▶ To add photos, click the **Add Photos** button and choose more photos to upload.

▶ To change who sees your album, click the audience selector drop-down arrow and choose another setting, such as Friends or a custom list.

▶ To make a photo the album cover, click the **Select an Option** drop-down arrow (see Figure 9.10) and choose **Make album cover**.

▶ To remove a photo you decide you don't want to include, click the **Select an Option** drop-down arrow (see Figure 9.10) and choose **Remove this photo**.

▶ To relocate the photo to another existing album, click the **Select an Option** drop-down arrow and choose **Move to other album**. If this is your first album, you won't see this option.

▶ To save all the changes you make to the Edit Album page, click the **Done** button located at the top of the page.

▶ If you click the **Delete Album** button at the top of the page, you can delete the entire album, photos and all. When activated, this option is permanent.

> NOTE: The photos you remove aren't really gone. They still exist somewhere in Facebook's storage servers. For that reason alone, always be careful about what photos you do post online, avoiding photos that embarrass, or ones that violate the site's terms of service. You may think someone cannot find them again, but they're still out there somewhere. It's better not even to post questionable photos in the first place. When in doubt, opt out!

Finally, the photo viewer window itself, shown in Figure 9.11, also offers a couple of editing options you can put to use. For example, does your photo need to be readjusted vertically or horizontally? Do you need to add a caption to a single photo? Do you want to tag a friend in a photo? You can do all of this from the photo viewer. From the album's page of thumbnails, click a photo to open the viewer window.

FIGURE 9.11   You can also edit individual photos using the photo viewer window.

Here are several editing options to pursue:

▶ To add a caption or change the date, click the **Edit** button and use the fields that appear to add a caption, set a new date, or change who can view your photo. Be sure to click the **Done Editing** button to save your changes.

▶ To tag a friend in the photo, click the **Tag Photo** button and follow the steps you learned in the previous section.

▶ To add a location, click the **Add Location** button and type in a location.

▶ To use the photo as your profile picture, click the drop-down arrow next to the tiny cog icon, as shown in Figure 9.12, and choose **Make Profile Picture**.

FIGURE 9.12   Click the drop-down arrow to view more editing options.

▶ If you're viewing a friend's photo in the viewer window, you can click the drop-down arrow (the tiny cog icon) and click **Download** to download the photo to your own computer.

▶ To remove a photo you decide you don't want to include, click the drop-down arrow and click **Delete this Photo**.

▶ To change a photo's orientation, click the drop-down arrow and click either **Rotate Left** or **Rotate Right**.

Summary

In this lesson, you learned how to upload and publish photos to share on Facebook. You learned how to tag people in a photo, use various uploaders, and edit albums. In the next lesson, you learn how to share videos.

LESSON 10

Sharing Videos

In this lesson, you learn how to share your own original video clips on Facebook. You'll learn how to upload, play, and record videos, and how to edit video information.

Sharing Videos on Facebook

You're not just limited to static images (that is, photos) on Facebook. You can also share videos. Whether you call them movies, videos, or multimedia clips, the result is still the same—a dynamic clip that you can play and watch. You can add videos to your timeline that, in turn, appear on the news feed of the Home page. You can also add videos to your notes and group pages, and even embed them on outside sites. As with photos, you can tag people in your videos, and add comments.

There are a few stipulations with using videos on Facebook, as follows:

- ▶ The video must be made by you or your friends.

- ▶ The video must be under 1024MB in size and less than 20 minutes in length. If you're a brand-new user, the limits may be smaller for you until you verify your account.

- ▶ The video should contain you or a friend.

Basically, you're not allowed to upload illegal copies of television shows, music videos, movies, or any content that's not made by you or a friend. The video content should be yours and yours alone. You're also expected to comply with Facebook's terms of service regarding the content you post. In other words, don't post copyrighted or pirated videos, or clips of questionable taste or subject matter. Facebook even makes you agree to this the first time you upload a video.

You can upload video clips you've previously recorded, such as videos from your camera or mobile device, or you can hook up your camera directly and record a new video. If your computer has a built-in camera and microphone, you can record directly from there. You can use Facebook's Video application for all of these options.

> TIP: To find out more about what's in Facebook's terms of service, you can click the **Terms** link at the very bottom of any Facebook page. To learn more, see Lesson 3, "Finding Help with Facebook Services and Etiquette."

Adding a Video

Adding a video is as easy as adding photos. Facebook has even grouped the Video app with the Photos app on the Photos page. So, any time you're looking for where your videos are located, start with the Photos link.

To add a previously recorded video to Facebook, follow these steps:

1. From your profile page, click the **Photos** link (it's located below the cover photo and your name). Facebook opens the Photos page and you can see the Add Videos button, as shown in Figure 10.1.

FIGURE 10.1   Look for the **Add Videos** button on the Photos page.

2. Click the **Add Videos** button. The Create a New Video page appears, as shown in Figure 10.2.

3. Click the **File Upload** tab, click the **Browse** or **Choose File** button, depending on your browser, and then navigate to and double-click the video file you want to upload.

4. If this is your first time uploading a video, Facebook displays an authorization box detailing the terms surrounding video use on Facebook. Click **Agree**.

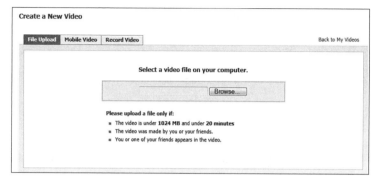

FIGURE 10.2   The first phase of uploading a video is locating it on your computer.

Facebook displays an information form, as shown in Figure 10.3, and the uploading process begins. Depending on your connection speed and file size, the process may take a few minutes. While waiting for the upload to finish, you can fill out the rest of the form.

Create a New Video

| File Upload | Mobile Video | Record Video | Back to My Videos |

Please wait while your video is uploading.

Cancel

1.21 MB of 4.61 MB (56.16 KB/sec) -- 1 minute remaining

Enter the following info while you wait for your upload to finish.

In this video:

Tag people who appear in this video.

Title:

Description:

Privacy: Friends

Save Info

FIGURE 10.3   Fill out a title and description for the clip and set a privacy level.

5. Click in the **Title** box and type a title for the video.

    Optionally, you can tag people who appear in the video using the In This Video box.

6. Click in the **Description** box and type a description for the video.

7. Click the **Privacy** drop-down menu and specify an audience level.

8. When the upload is complete, click the **Save Info** button. Note: the upload may take several moments or minutes, depending on size and connection speeds.

9. The video now appears on the Your Videos page, as shown in Figure 10.4, as well as on your profile page's timeline and in the news feed on the Home page. To play the clip, move the mouse over the clip and click the **Play** button.

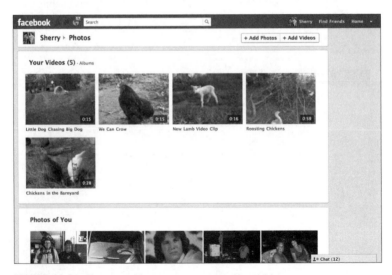

FIGURE 10.4   The new video appears on the Your Videos page.

You can also upload a video clip from your mobile device or record a clip using your computer's built-in camera recorder. On the Create a New Video page, click the **Mobile Video** or **Record Video** tabs. Learn how to record a new video later in this lesson. Learn more about using Facebook's mobile features in Lesson 16, "Making Facebook Mobile."

NOTE: You can also upload videos using your Update Status box on the Home page or on your profile page. From the Home page, click the **Add Photo/Video** link above the status box. From your profile page, click the **Photo** link in the status box, and then click the **Upload Photo/Video**. The rest of the steps are the same as outlined here.

Viewing Videos

Videos your friends post appear out on the news feed on the Home page, as well as on their timelines. You can play a video clip directly in the news feed by clicking its **Play** button, as shown in Figure 10.5. This enables you to view the clip without opening it in its own window.

FIGURE 10.5   You can play videos directly in the news feed on the Home page by clicking the Play button on the video's thumbnail image.

If you move your mouse pointer over the bottom of the video image while the clip is playing, a bar of player controls appears (see Figure 10.6). The player has controls for pausing the clip, muting the clip, or showing it full-screen size. The controls appear only when the clip is playing.

FIGURE 10.6　You can move your mouse over the bottom of a clip to view player controls.

Here's how to use the player controls:

► Click the **Pause** button to stop the clip. When the pause action is in effect, the **Play** button appears in its place to start the clip again.

► To mute the clip, click the **speaker** icon.

► To adjust the sound, drag the audio level up or down.

► To view the clip in a full-size window, click the **window** icon on the far-right end of the player controls.

If you do want to play a video in its own window, click the video title link next to the thumbnail image.

If you're viewing a friend's profile page and she has a video clip, you can click the **Play** button to view the clip in her timeline. To share the video clip with someone else, click the **Share** link to open the Share box. You can choose to post the clip to your own profile for sharing, or send it as a message. You can find this same **Share** link on the news feed on the Home page, too.

You and your friends can add comments to your video clip in the same way comments are added to photos: using a Comment box. You can add comments directly to a clip on the news feed by clicking the **Comment** link to open a Comment box and typing in your text. You can also add a comment to a video from its video window by clicking in the **Comment** box below the video image and typing in your text.

To find your way back to your own videos, open your profile page and click the **Photos** link, and then click the **Videos** link on the Photos page. The page lists all the videos you've posted. To play one, click the video to open it in its own window and click the **Play** button.

Editing Your Videos

To edit a video and change the description or title, or tag the subjects, you need to open the video in its own window. One way to do this is to display the Your Videos page (click the **Photos** link on your profile page, and then click the **Videos** link). As you've previously learned, the Your Videos page, shown in Figure 10.7, lists your video postings. Click the video you want to edit, opening it into its own window as shown in Figure 10.8.

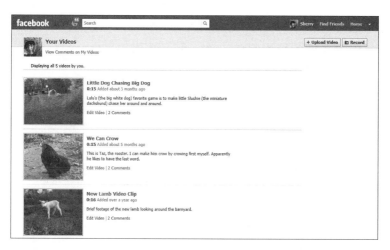

FIGURE 10.7   Your Videos page shows all your uploaded videos.

FIGURE 10.8   You can open a larger window to view a video clip and find controls for editing.

From the video window, you can do the following:

▶ Click the **Edit This Video** link below the video player and make changes to the information, such as give it a new title or description.

▶ Click the **Tag This Video** link to open a field below the player area where you can type in the name of the person you're tagging. Click the **Save** button when you finish.

▶ Click the **Delete Video** link to remove the video entirely. You'll have to confirm the removal by clicking the **Delete** button that appears when Facebook warns you that the deletion is permanent.

▶ You can use the rotation icons to rotate the video clockwise or counterclockwise, if needed.

▶ Click the **Embed this Video** link to open an Embed Your Video box containing the coding needed to embed the video on any web page. Just copy and paste the coding.

Recording a New Video

If your computer has a built-in camera and microphone, or if you have a digital video recorder you can hook up to your computer, you can record your own video clips to post on Facebook. With a little help from Adobe's Flash Player, you can record and place the clips directly into Facebook, where they can be viewed on your profile page as well as the news feed out on the Home page.

Follow these steps to record a new video:

1. Display the Your Videos or Your Photos page and click the **Add Videos** button.

   Facebook displays the Create a New Video form, which you learned about earlier (refer to Figure 10.3).

2. Click the **Record Video** tab.

   Flash displays a tiny Flash Player Settings dialog box in the middle, as shown in Figure 10.9, requesting to allow Facebook access to your camera. If you've uploaded video before, you might not see this box.

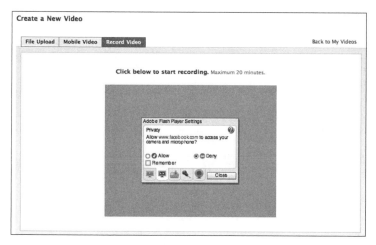

FIGURE 10.9 Before you start recording, you must allow Facebook access to your camera.

3. Depending on the box you see, which can vary based on your browser, click the **Allow** radio button or the **Allow** check box.

4. Depending on your prompt box, you might need to close it to continue; click **Close**.

5. When you're ready to start recording, click the **Record** button, as shown in Figure 10.10.

| File Upload | Mobile Video | Record Video | | Back to My Videos |

Click below to start recording. Maximum 20 minutes.

FIGURE 10.10   Click **Record** and yell "action," and the movie is rolling, so to speak.

6. Click the **Stop** button to stop recording (see Figure 10.11). Facebook displays more video controls, as shown in Figure 10.12.

   If the recording did not go well, you can click the **Reset** button and try again.

7. If you've finished recording, click the **Save** button. Facebook displays a form for filling out details about the video recording, as shown in Figure 10.13.

FIGURE 10.11   Click the **Stop** button to stop at any time.

FIGURE 10.12   When you stop recording, more video controls appear on the page, allowing you to reset and start over again, or to save what you've recorded.

FIGURE 10.13   Fill out details about your video recording using the form.

8. If applicable, enter any names of friends (or yourself) to tag people in the video using the In This Video box.

9. Type a name for the video in the Title box.

10. Type a description of the video in the Description box. Optionally, you can choose a different thumbnail image for the video's "cover" to represent the video.

11. Click the **Privacy** drop-down arrow and choose an audience setting for the video.

12. Click the **Save** button, and Facebook saves the recording and adds it to your video list.

You can return to the Your Videos page to view the recording. Facebook also automatically adds it to your timeline and the news feed, too.

Summary

In this lesson, you learned how to share your video clips on Facebook. You learned how to upload existing clips, record new clips, and view clips found all over Facebook. In the next lesson, you'll learn how to join Facebook groups and even start your own groups.

LESSON 11

Joining Groups

In this lesson, you learn how to find and join Facebook groups. You'll learn how to search for groups of interest, join a group, view group pages, and even create and manage your own group.

Socializing with Facebook Groups

Yet another way to socialize and network on Facebook is through groups. You can use Facebook groups to mix and mingle with people outside your Friends list and make new friends along the way. You can also use groups to share information with a specific set of people, such as family members, coworkers, and teammates. Groups are gathering places generally organized around a common interest, such as a hobby, a favorite topic, or a cause. Groups on Facebook run the gamut from silly to serious, and finding all kinds of humorous groups to join just for the fun of it is not uncommon, especially those attempting to break a record or participate in some type of social experiment. Need to agonize with someone over your ongoing shoe-shopping problem? There's a group for that. Do you want to commiserate with fellow foodies over the quest for a good steak? There's a group for that. Do you want to link up with fellow aircraft enthusiasts or civil war buffs? There are groups for both. The possibilities are endless and waiting for you to explore, and you'll quickly see that a huge number of groups are out there.

Groups are the perfect venue for sharing ideas, passions, social and political issues, or just creating a place to connect. You can learn a lot from specialty subject groups, or find an avenue to post questions to others about a topic you want to know more about. Chances are, you'll find somebody willing to offer information in no time at all.

You can search for different kinds of groups, as well as create your own group. You're bound to find a group to suit your needs. For example, if

you're into politics, you can find a group based around your political leanings, or if you're a reality TV show addict, you can find a group of fellow
fans to share news. Many companies, politicians, celebrities, musicians,
and even products have avid groups going on Facebook as well as on their
Pages. (Learn the difference between groups and Pages in Lesson 14,
"Understanding Pages.") You can even find groups about Facebook itself.
If you can't find a group for your topic of interest, you can create your
own group and invite others to join.

Groups can attract hundreds or thousands of people, or just a few. Groups
form to air grievances, express ideologies, or just gush about a favorite
actor or band. Groups can also be a powerful tool to spread a message,
organizing people into grassroots movements, social causes, and more.
Election years create a lot of groups on Facebook, as you can imagine.
Figure 11.1 shows an example of a group my friend started because we all
dabble in photography. Each week the group members share photos surrounding a specified theme.

FIGURE 11.1   An example of a typical group page on Facebook.

Groups are run by an administrator, usually the person who created the
group. Larger groups may also include additional administrators to help

manage the postings. Depending on the group and what's allowed, group members can share comments, participate in group chat, and post photos, videos, links, share docs (dynamic wiki-like documents everyone can add to and edit), and so on.

Facebook groups are divided into three main types, as follows:

▶ **Open**—Open groups are public, which means anyone can see the group and its members' postings. Open groups allow anyone on Facebook to join. You can request to join, and after you're accepted, you can invite your friends.

▶ **Closed**—Closed groups are visible in a search, but you cannot view any member postings. Closed groups are more exclusive and require an invitation to join. You can also ask to join a closed group, and it's up to the administrator to let you in or not.

▶ **Secret**—Secret groups are not advertised anywhere on Facebook, and can only be joined by invitation.

In October 2011, Facebook redesigned groups to facilitate better sharing, such as group docs, group chat, and improved notifications. Prior to the change, groups utilized their own profile pages and appeared as regular profiles. The new group format displays the group and its postings more like a news feed, similar to the main Home page.

Now that you know a little about groups, it's time to find groups and join up.

CAUTION: Watch out for spammers! Finding spamming going on among the larger open Facebook groups, such as people selling products and services or get-rich schemes, is not uncommon. Although spamming isn't allowed on Facebook, it still occurs. You can report a spam posting by clicking the **Report/Mark as Spam** link found when you click the drop-down arrow next to the posting.

NOTE: Older groups created before October 2011 do not feature the new group design and elements. If the group was not very active, Facebook automatically archived the group. If the group experiences an influx of new activity, it can upgrade to the new format. To learn more about how to convert an old group to a new group, visit Facebook's Help Center.

Finding a Group

One way to find a group is to pay attention to the news feed on the Home page to see what groups your friends are joining. If you see something interesting, check it out. You might also spot an interesting group to join while perusing your friends' profiles. For serious group exploration, however, you can conduct a search.

You can use the Search field at the top of any Facebook page to search for a specific topic. For example, if you want to find a group related to snow skiing in Colorado or a moms group in your area, you can conduct a quick search and see what's available. There are groups centered on just about every subject you can think of, and many more you hadn't thought of at all. Simply click in the **Search** field and type the keyword or words you want to search for. By default, Facebook lists the top few results in a drop-down list as soon as you type a word. Scroll down the results list that appears and click the **See more results** link at the bottom. This opens a page displaying all the results, as shown in Figure 11.2, including filters on the left for choosing which type of results you want to view. In this case, click the **Groups** filter to view only groups.

The results page for groups lists the groups with a block of information detailing the group name, number of members, and type of group. To view a group, click the group name to open its page. The group page tells you more about the group, and you can see what sort of activities they pursue. If it's an open group, you can view postings other group members have added. If it's a closed group, you can only view the basic info about the group. See the next section to learn more about joining groups.

Joining a Group

You can join up to 300 groups on Facebook, so don't feel limited to just a few. After you find a group that interests you, ask to join it and become a member. Checking out the group page first is a good idea just to see

whether it's something you really want to participate in, as shown in
Figure 11.3. Group pages can include features found on regular profile
pages, including a profile picture, a news feed wall, posted links, photos
and videos, and a listing of members.

FIGURE 11.2   You can use the search feature to help you look for groups
on Facebook.

You can view the various postings to get an idea of how the group operates.
You should also check to see whether the group has active postings based
on dates. If the last posting was six months ago, the group probably isn't,
uh, thriving.

If you're ready to join, and it's an open group, look for the **Ask to Join**
button on the group's page and click it. The group administrator then has
to approve the request, if applicable. If this is the case, you'll need to
check back and see whether you're accepted. Depending on how the group
is administrated, you might not necessarily need approval before joining.

If the group is closed, you can join only if the administrator of the group
allows you to; you'll still have to request to join, just as with an open group.

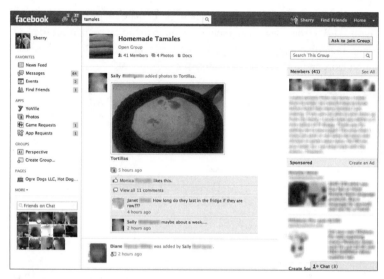

FIGURE 11.3   A typical group page.

A new feature to groups is automatic joining. Your friends can automatically add you to the membership ranks if the group is an open group type. For example, when a friend joins an open group without administrator restrictions or creates a new group, he or she has the option to specify other Facebook friends in the process. If you find yourself a member of a group you do not want to belong to, you can always leave the group. From the group page, look for the cog-like icon in the upper-right corner (next to the Notifications button); click it and select **Leave Group** from the drop-down menu.

After you've joined a group, you can start participating. Communication in groups takes place mainly in the news feed area of the Wall. Look for the Write Something box to add your own input, including posts, photos or videos, or polling questions. Groups can also communicate through group chats and group emails.

Groups you join appear in an abbreviated list under the **Groups** heading on the far-left side of your Home page. To visit a group, just click its name. You can also open the Groups page, a page listing all the groups you've joined on Facebook. To access this special page, click the **Groups** heading label on the Home page.

Starting Your Own Group

Creating a group on Facebook is easier than ever. You might want to build a group around a particular hobby, or make a group for an interest in your area or region of the country. You might also create a new group to serve a specific purpose, such as a work group centered around a project, or a family group focused just on your family members. Before you jump in and make a new group, take a few minutes to figure out these details first:

▶ **Decide** what you want to name the group. Watch out for misspellings and typos!

▶ **Decide** what photo you want to use as the group profile picture. Try to choose an image that goes along with what the group is about.

▶ **Write** out a brief description of the group, stating the group's purpose, mission, or intent.

▶ **Formulate** an idea about what type of group you're creating, such as common interest, business related, or just for fun.

▶ **Decide** on availability: open, closed, or secret.

▶ If you're creating an open group, decide whether you want to administrate membership approval. Some people prefer not having to deal with requests to join the group.

You'll save yourself some time and effort by organizing your group information before actually creating the group.

To start your own group, follow these steps from the Groups page:

1. From the Home page, click the **Group** heading label over in the left pane. Facebook displays the Groups page, similar to the one shown in Figure 11.4.

2. Click the **Create Group** button. The Create Group form opens, shown in Figure 11.5.

3. Click in the **Group Name** box and type in a name.

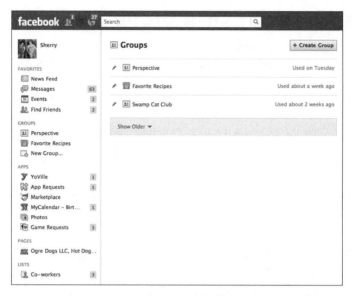

FIGURE 11.4   The Groups page lists all the groups you've joined on Facebook.

FIGURE 11.5   Fill out the form with a group name, privacy group type, and list anyone you want to include automatically in the group.

Optionally, you can click the icon drop-down list in the Group Name field and choose an icon that represents the type of group you're making.

4. To add specific Facebook friends to your group, click in the **Members** box and start typing names. Facebook displays a pop-up list and you can choose friends. You can add as many as you want.

5. Click a Privacy option for the group: Open, Closed, or Secret.

6. Click the **Create** button. Facebook displays the new group page, as shown in Figure 11.6.

FIGURE 11.6   Behold, a new group page.

The next phase to creating a group is to edit the group settings. This includes assigning a profile picture, deciding whether you want to approve requests to join, setting up a group email, and filling out a description. You can tackle all these options from the Edit page. To view the page, click the cog-like icon next to the Notifications button (see Figure 11.7), and select **Edit Group** from the menu that appears. Figure 11.8 shows the group settings for the new group I just created.

FIGURE 11.7   Use the drop-down menu to find editing options for your group page.

FIGURE 11.8   Use this page to add more details and settings to your group.

Take a few moments to scroll up and down the page to view the various settings and controls. As the group administrator, you can choose from the following options:

▶ To assign a profile picture, click the **Choose File** or **Browse** button under the Profile Picture area or use your computer's camera to take a new picture. You might want to use this opportunity to add a picture that illustrates your group's purpose or identity.

▶ If you ever need to change the group name, you can do so in the **Group Name** box on this page. In the past, you were stuck with whatever name you assigned when you first made the group. Now, you can tweak it, if needed, based on member input.

▶ You can also change the group's privacy setting to something else. For example, you might have started with an open group but decide later to close it to just the current members. You can do this only with groups that have fewer than 250 people.

▶ As the administrator, you can choose to approve all requests to join or not. Click the **Membership Approval** check box if you want to control who joins the group. If the group is open and you do not select this check box, anyone can join without needing approval.

▶ You can use the **Email Address** option to set up a group email address for communicating with everyone in the group through a specific email address in Facebook.

▶ Use the **Description** box to type up a description of your group, such as its purpose, expectations, and so on.

▶ As administrator, you can also control who can post items on the group Wall.

After you complete the edits, be sure to click the **Save** button at the bottom of the page to keep your changes and apply them to the group. Click the **Back to Wall** link at the top of the Edit page to return to the group page.

Managing Your Group

As the creator of a group, you're in charge of administering the group. You're automatically given the title of administrator, also called *admin* for short on Facebook. Keeping an eye on the group and the content posted there by others and keeping the group alive and active are your jobs. You can post news about the group, send out group messages to your members, create events, docs, and so forth. Basically, this is your club, and you're in charge of making everyone feel welcome and encouraging participation.

You can change the profile picture just as you do on a regular profile page. You can find links to tasks you can do to manage the group located directly below the group's profile picture, as shown in Figure 11.9. You can also return to the form fields you originally filled out to create the group and make changes to the information.

FIGURE 11.9   Use the links on the group page to manage the group.

Here are a few management tasks you can do on your group's page:

► To share photos or videos, click the **Add Photo/Video** link in the Write Something box on the group page and upload the file(s).

► To ask a polling question, click the **Ask Question** link in the Write Something box and ask your question. You can then use the polling options link to include specific answer choices.

► To view all the photos posted by the group, click the **Photos** link beneath the group name to open a page listing photos.

► To view your members list, similar to the list shown in Figure 11.10, click the members link beneath the group name. You can also click the **See All** link over on the right side of the page next to the Members heading.

FIGURE 11.10 The Members page lists all the group's members, and includes options for removing members and assigning administrator status.

▶ To chat with everyone at the same time, click the cog-like icon (refer to Figure 11.7) in the upper-right corner of the group page and select **Chat with Group**. To learn more about the chat feature, see Lesson 6, "Connecting with Friends."

▶ To add more people to your group, display the members list again and click the **Add Friends** button in the upper-right corner. This opens a box where you can type the names of other Facebook friends you want to add to the group.

▶ To create a group doc, click the **Docs** link beneath the group name and type up your document contents.

▶ To make someone an administrator, open the Members list and click the **Make Admin** button next to the person's name. You can use the same process to remove admin status.

▶ You can also create events for your group. See Lesson 12, "Tracking Events," to learn more about this Facebook feature.

NOTE: When you create a group-related event, it shows up on the group's page and all the group members are invited to attend.

Along with the management activities described previously, you can also administer the postings on the Wall:

▶ To remove a post from the Wall, click the drop-down arrow next to the posting, and then click **Delete Post**, as shown in Figure 11.11. Confirm the deletion to make it permanent.

FIGURE 11.11   You can easily remove a post from the group using the Delete Post feature.

▶ To remove a member from the group, open the Members list and click the **X** button next to the person's name. Facebook prompts you to confirm the removal; click **Confirm**. If he wants back in the group again, he must request to join.

▶ To permanently remove someone from your group and not allow him back, you can activate the Ban Permanently feature. When you delete the person and confirm his removal, click the **Ban Permanently** check box before clicking **Confirm**. The person can no longer find the group in a Facebook search, see group content, or request to rejoin.

TIP: To delete your group from Facebook, remove all the members, including yourself. If you prefer to exit the group yourself but leave it active and give it to someone else to manage, you can assign admin status to another member.

Summary

In this lesson, you learned how to utilize groups on Facebook. You learned how to look for groups to join, how to manage the groups you join, and how to create brand-new groups and act as administrator. In the next lesson, you learn how to use Facebook events.

Tracking Events

In this lesson, you learn how to work with Facebook events. You learn how to search for events in your area and handle event invitations. You also learn how to create your own events and manage their pages.

Events Overview

Events are another amazing social aspect of using Facebook. You can quickly get the word out among your friends and interested others about upcoming events, whether it's a party, a concert, a trip, or any other kind of social gathering. For example, if you're organizing a rally of some sort, you can turn it into a Facebook event to let everyone know about it and invite people to attend and spread the word, thus increasing your chances of a good crowd. In another example, a friend of a friend might be having a backyard barbecue, and you don't know whether you want to go or not. You can check the attendees list to see whether anyone else you know is going. Facebook events are perfect for sending out informal invitations and planning out your social itinerary.

You can use Facebook's Events application to advertise an event, track attendees, view birthdays, and find other events. The application is one of several default applications already loaded into your Facebook account. You can use the application to search for events in your area, or create new events yourself. The Events application acts as your personal secretary with regard to your social calendar.

You can use the Events application to create all kinds of events, including numerous types of parties, fundraisers, meetings, educational classes or study groups, exhibits, recitals, sporting events and tournaments, trips, and festivals. Events you create using the Events application have their own pages on Facebook. The person who creates the event page in Facebook is the page's administrator and controls the content and management of the event page. An event page, shown in Figure 12.1, looks similar to a group page and features information about the event itself. It has an area listing details and a description, an event "profile" picture area, a Wall for posting comments, and features for tracking who's attending and how to RSVP.

FIGURE 12.1   An example of a typical event page on Facebook.

Facebook events come in two different types, as follows:

▶ **Public Events**—Anyone can read about a public event and accept an invitation to attend it. Public events are perfect for festivals, gallery showings, concerts, and other large public gatherings.

▶ **Private Events**—Only the people you invite can choose to attend a private event.

Whether you can attend an event or not depends on how it is listed. Look in the Event Type area of the page to see what type of event it is.

There are also a few things to keep in mind when attending Facebook events in person. Meeting people online and meeting them face to face are both situations in which you should always use common sense coupled with caution. Just because someone appears to be one way online doesn't mean he or she will be the same in person. Online dangers can often be avoided by following secure habits (antivirus software, privacy settings, passwords, and so on); however, when you meet people in real life, criminal behaviors can take physical shape. Just be careful!

Finding Events

Ready to find something fun to do? Or how about seeing what your friends are attending? You can find out about an event in several ways. One way is to check the news feed on the Home page to see what events your friends are attending. You can also search for specific events.

On the Home page, you can view upcoming events on the right side of the page just above all the advertising. You can use the Events page to view a list of all the events you've responded to or are invited to. To access the app, just click the **Events** link on the left side of the Home page. Facebook opens the Events page, shown in Figure 12.2.

FIGURE 12.2   Use the Events page to view your events.

You can use this page to view events by month and make use of the following links at the bottom of the listing:

- ▶ **Past Events**—Displays an archive of previous events.
- ▶ **Declined Events**—Displays events you've declined.
- ▶ **Birthdays**—Displays all your Facebook friends with upcoming birthdays.
- ▶ **Export**—Exports your events to another scheduling program, such as Microsoft Outlook or Google Calendar.

Also at the top of the Events page is a **Create Event** button for making your own event listings.

Searching for an Event

If you know the event you're looking for, either by name or subject, you can use the built-in search tool to look it up. To conduct a search, click in the **Search** box at the top of the Facebook page.

Type in the word or words you want to search for. As you type, Facebook displays a drop-down menu with any matching results, similar to those shown in Figure 12.3. Click the **See More Results** option at the bottom of the menu to open a search results page, as shown in Figure 12.4. Click the **Events** filter on the left side of the page to display just events in the results and not just any Facebook page.

FIGURE 12.3   You can use the search feature to look for specific events.

FIGURE 12.4   Filter your search results to show only events.

When you see an event that matches what you want, you can click the event name to view the event's page. You can find out more about the event, see who is attending, and locate a link to RSVP yourself.

Responding to an Event

To sign up to attend an event, click the **Join** button on the event's page, as shown in Figure 12.5. This immediately adds your name and a thumbnail of your profile picture under the Going category located on the left side of the event page.

If you're not attending, click the **Decline** button. If you're still undecided, click the **Maybe** option, which adds your name under the Maybe category. In the past, Facebook events utilized the common RSVP lingo to interact with events to which you're invited, including buttons for attending and not attending. With the latest Facebook interface, the event response buttons are labeled **Join**, **Maybe**, and **Decline**.

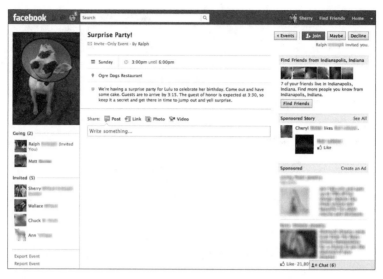

FIGURE 12.5   Use the response buttons to let the page administrator know whether you're attending.

Meanwhile, back on the Events page, you can quickly see whether you're attending an event, and you can even join an event without having to open the event's profile page.

You can also change an RSVP response from the event's profile page. For example, if you originally said you were attending, but now you need to cancel, you can open the profile page, click the **Going** button, and change your response. If you originally declined an invitation, you can open it again through your Events page by clicking the **Past Events** link and revisiting the event page from there.

Creating Your Own Events

You can create your own events and invite others to join you. Events run the full gamut from public gatherings to intimate parties. For example, if you're part of a group organizing a "fun run" race or other fundraising event, you can create a Facebook event and invite people to attend. After people start responding, their friends see the event, and they think about attending, too. It's great word of mouth about your group and your cause. Facebook events are perfect for advertising festivals, flea markets, gallery openings, holiday parties, business meetings, conventions, piano recitals, tournaments, workshops, and so on.

Before you begin creating a new event, take a moment and figure out the details you'll need for posting the event. Required data includes a name for the event and a date and time. You cannot create an event without this information. You'll also need some basic information, such as the location of the event. Although it's not a requirement, having a picture handy to go along with your event page—something that illustrates what the event is about or the organization hosting the event—is a good idea.

When you're ready to create an event, follow these steps:

1. Open the Events page (by clicking the **Events** link on the Home page).

2. Click the **Create Event** button. Facebook opens a form you can fill out to create the event, as shown in Figure 12.6.

3. Click in the **Event Name** box and type a name for the event.

FIGURE 12.6   To create a new event, fill out this form page.

4. Click the **Date and Time** boxes to set the date, start time, and (optionally) end time.

5. Click in the **Location** box and type a location.

6. Click in the **Details** box and type all the details surrounding the event. Details can include instructions for guests, directions, or any other info you need to convey or explain about the event.

7. To invite friends, click the **Select Guests** button to display the Invite Friends dialog box, shown in Figure 12.7.

FIGURE 12.7   Use this dialog box to invite your friends to the event.

8. Select which friends you want to invite, and then click the **Save and Close** button.

    Optionally, you can add a personal message to the invitation by clicking the **Add a Personal Message** link and typing the message.

    You can also invite people outside your Facebook circle; just type the email addresses in the **Invite by E-mail Address** box.

CAUTION: You can only invite 100 people at a time. If you need to invite more, use the Invite Friends link found on the event's profile page.

9. Choose whether you want the event to be public or private. Deselect the **Make This Event Public** check box to make the event private.

To include the guest list on the event's profile page, leave the **Show the Guest List on the Event Page** check box selected.

10. To add a photo to the page, click the **Add Event Photo** link and upload a picture.

11. Click the **Create Event** button at the bottom of the form.

Facebook displays the event page and sends out your invitations.

Managing Your Events

After you've created an event, you're automatically the administrator of the event page. This means you can edit the page's info, make changes to the guest list, and send out more invitations as needed.

To view the page at any time, open the event's profile page. Here's what you can do:

▶ To edit the page, just click the **Edit** button. This opens the same form you used to create the event, and you can make changes to the information.

▶ To invite more people to come, click the **Invite Friends** link and select more Facebook friends to invite.

▶ To send a message to attendees, such as a reminder about the date, click the cog-like icon and select **Message Guests**.

▶ To cancel the event, click the cog-like icon and select **Cancel This Event** to open a prompt box; click **Yes**. Facebook notifies everyone on your guest list. Canceling is a one-time deal—you cannot undo it and "uncancel" the event again.

You can continue monitoring your event page leading up to the event, checking to see who is attending, not attending, or thinking about attending, and viewing any page content left by the invitees. You can send out messages to the attendees. You can also update the page with the latest news about the event as it draws near.

Summary

In this lesson, you learned how to find and create events on Facebook. You learned how to look for events to attend, and how to create a new event and invite your friends. You also learned how to respond to event invitations and administer an event page. In the next lesson, you'll learn how to use Facebook applications.

LESSON 13
Adding Applications

In this lesson, you learn how to use applications to enhance your Facebook experience. You'll learn how to search for applications and add interesting ones to your collection. You'll also learn how to manage your applications, edit their settings, and remove apps you no longer want.

What Are Apps?

Applications are tiny programs that run within the Facebook environment—also called *apps* for short. Applications are similar to plug-ins you use to enhance your web browser, but in the case of Facebook, they enhance your social networking experiences. You've already been using applications on Facebook, perhaps without even knowing it, and we've covered quite a few so far in this book. This section will go into them with a bit more detail.

As you know, Facebook has several default applications going as soon as you create your account. If you've posted your status, uploaded a photo or video, created a group or event, emailed a message, or chatted online, you've used a Facebook app. Apps work seamlessly within the Facebook interface.

Facebook's designers have included many useful built-in apps, but literally hundreds of applications exist that you can add to your Facebook experience. Some are quite useful, and some are just for fun. These additional applications are created by third-party developers. Facebook has allowed third-party developers free access to the Facebook platform for several years now, so anyone who has some programming experience or where-withal can write an application for the site. Because of this freedom, Facebook is literally swarming with apps, and many of them are quite clever and creative. You can use as many as you want, and discard those you do not care for after giving them a whirl. All the extra apps you add, however, require your authorization to access your Facebook profile data. In many respects, adding an application is similar to adding a friend to your Friends list. Apps are part of your Facebook account until you discard them. In many cases, apps publish your application activities on your profile page and out in the main news feed. This lets your friends know what applications you use and might inspire them to use them, too—all part of the viral spread of apps on Facebook.

CAUTION: When you allow an application access to your profile, it accesses all of your information and that of your friends, too. If you're worried about privacy, applications might not be your cup of tea. For this very reason, you might not want to include too much personal information on your Facebook pages. (To learn more about privacy settings, see Lesson 7, "Guarding Your Privacy.") You can, however, control some of the invasiveness of apps through the application's settings. Learn more about editing apps later in this lesson.

TIP: If you want to learn how to create your own apps for Facebook, check out the Developers page for more information, tips, and help. Click the **Developers** link at the bottom of any Facebook page to investigate further.

Kinds of Apps

At this point, you might be wondering what kinds of things apps offer. A wide variety of applications are available, ranging from business and education to fun and games. For example, culture-sharing apps let you share information about things that interest you and your friends, such as musical tastes, books you just read, or movie reviews. Friendship apps include applications designed to organize and interact with friends. Game apps let you play interactive or single-player games.

One of the more popular apps is FamilyLink's *We're Related*, an application to help you locate and connect with relatives around the globe.

Another popular application just for fun is *Flixter*, which helps you and your friends compare movie tastes. Some apps create digital worlds where you can interact with other people, such as *FarmVille* (the most popular app on Facebook), *YoVille* (see Figure 13.1), or *Mafia Wars* (all created by Zynga games), whereas other apps enhance a popular Facebook activity, such as *Birthday Cards* (sending electronic birthday cards to friends) or *MyCalendar* (for helping you keep track of birthdays).

FIGURE 13.1 In *YoVille*, you can wander around a digital world collecting coins and shopping for stuff for your digital dwelling, as well as interacting with your Facebook friends who also exist in *YoVille*.

NOTE: Facebook applications are free to use; however, some apps ask for donations for a cause or offer additional privileges for a small fee, such as games. You can decide whether to pursue these extra costs.

Finding Apps

You can encounter applications in several ways on Facebook. Friends might send you an app request, such as a game application in which they invite you to play or interact with them, or a "gift" you must then use the application to view. Application requests typically occur when a friend adds a new application to their repertoire, and it asks to add you, as well, because you're on their Friends list. Application requests show up in the App Requests link on your Home page (left side of the page under the Apps heading). As you learned back in Lesson 5, "Navigating the Home Page," all of your Facebook notifications show up in the left pane of the Home page.

Speaking of the Home page, you might notice your Facebook friends playing games or using apps by the listings that appear over on the ticker, the real-time scrollable list that appears in the upper-right corner of the Home page. This is another area to observe with regard to checking out what apps your friends are using. This same ticker also appears when you're playing apps, and lists similar stories from your friends.

You can also encounter apps on other people's profile pages. If you see something you think you would enjoy, you can click the application name in the story posting to learn more about the application.

Finally, you can use Facebook's Apps Dashboard to browse for apps or use Facebook's Search tool to look for specific ones to learn more about them. The Apps Dashboard, itself an application, lets you browse for apps based on recommended Facebook apps, new apps, or apps your friends are using.

Deciding which apps are right for you is really a personal preference. Many of the Facebook apps are viral, quickly spreading in popularity as they're shared among friends—your friend adds the application, it looks interesting, so you add it, too. If you see an app you want to try, you can check out its page first to learn more about it and find out which of your friends is using the app.

Responding to an App Request

Basically, an application request is when an app invites you to participate
in whatever it's about, or when your friend who uses the app wants to
invite you to use it, too. When you receive an application request, it
appears in the left pane area of your Home page listed next to the **App
Requests** link, as shown in Figure 13.2. If you receive a game request, it
appears next to the **Game Requests** link. Click **App Requests** to view the
Apps page, as shown in Figure 13.3.

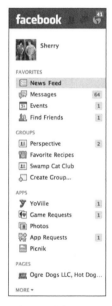

FIGURE 13.2   Look for app requests under the Apps heading on your Home
page.

The top of the Apps page displays your requests. (Learn about the bottom
of the Apps page in the next section.) You can respond to a request in several ways:

▶ The first option, though it might have different names, is essentially a button you can click to join, accept, or participate. In
Figure 13.3, for example, I can click the **Accept** button to add the
app to my Facebook collection. When clicked, additional pages
may open where you can allow the application to access your data.

FIGURE 13.3   The Apps page lists any of the app requests you've received from friends, along with recommendations from Facebook.

- ▶ The second option is to remove the request by clicking the **Delete** button (X).

- ▶ A third option may be just to ignore the request. Look for an **Ignore** or **Ignore All** link and click it.

If you prefer to learn more about the application before choosing a request response, you can visit the app's info or "profile" page and learn more about it. Move your mouse pointer over the app name that appears in the request area to view a pop-up box; click the app name in the box to go directly to the app's profile page. Similar to a regular profile page, an application's profile, shown in Figure 13.4, offers basic information, a Wall for comments, and even a profile picture. Also on the app's profile page, you'll find another button for adding the app if you decide you need to install it; click **Go to App** to start the procedure.

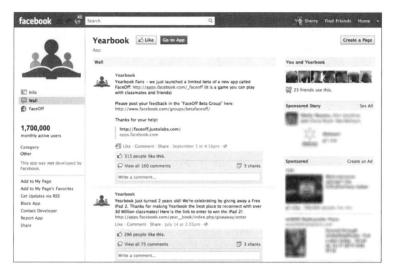

FIGURE 13.4   Learn more about an app by viewing its profile page.

When you do decide to add an app, a Request for Permission page appears, similar to the one shown in Figure 13.5. If you agree with the permissions requested, click the **Allow** button and add the app. If you don't agree, click the **Don't Allow** button instead.

FIGURE 13.5   Before you add an app, you'll need to give it permission to access your Facebook data.

Apps you add appear listed on your Home page under the Apps heading, with the most-used apps in view, or you can see a full list by actually clicking the **Apps** heading label.

Browsing Apps with the Apps Dashboard

Time to talk about the bottom portion of the Apps page, shown in Figure 13.6; with literally hundreds of apps to choose from, finding apps is easier when you can just view a few from a top picks list. To see a sampling of top picks, scroll to the bottom portion of the Apps Dashboard (also known as the Apps page) and browse among the recommendations, new apps, or a list of apps your friends are using. As mentioned in the previous section, you can display the page simply by clicking the **Apps Request** link. If the link isn't visible, click the **More** link next to the Apps heading, and then click the **App Request** link on the page that appears.

FIGURE 13.6   The bottom portion of the Apps page lists recommended apps, new apps, and apps your friends are using.

Click the **Recommended Apps** tab to view a list of Facebook-recommended apps. To see a sampling of new apps, click the **Newest** tab. To see what apps your friends are using, click the **Friends Using** tab. From any of the apps that appear, you can click an app name to add it. If you want to check it out first, click the app's link name on the Request for Permission page.

Using Keywords to Search for Apps

You can also conduct a keyword search to look for a specific application. Simply type in the keyword or words you want to search for in the Search box at the top of any Facebook page and click the **See More Results** link at the bottom of the pop-up menu that appears.

On the results page, click the **Apps** filter to view just the apps that match your search criteria.

Managing Apps

After you've added an application, you can use it as much or as little as you want. Depending on the app, you can change how it's accessed. You can control apps through the Apps Settings page. (See the next section to learn more.) Some apps even let you put a bookmark icon on the Home page for quicker access.

Changing Application Settings

You can edit your applications through the Apps Settings page, shown in Figure 13.7. To navigate to the page, click the drop-down arrow next to the Home button on any Facebook page and click **Account Settings**. This opens the Account Settings page. Click the **Apps** link on the left side of the page to display the Apps Settings.

The Apps Settings page lists each of the applications you are using.

To edit an application from your list, click the **Edit** link. This displays an area detailing the app's activities and settings. For example, in Figure 13.8, the *YoVille* app settings tell me what data I have allowed it to access. Depending on the application, you might be able to change privacy settings, add a bookmark, or control how related stories are generated when using the application. To control who sees your app activities, click the **Audience Selector** drop-down list and choose an audience, such as a custom friends list. Click **Close** to close out the app's details.

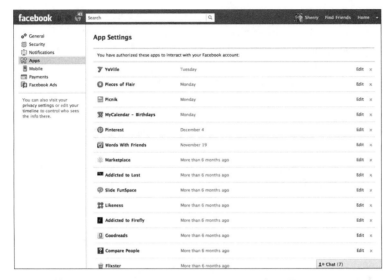

FIGURE 13.7   Use the Apps Setting page to control your Facebook apps.

FIGURE 13.8   You can view each app's details and change the settings, as needed.

To view more information about the application, click the app's name link. This takes you to the app's profile page, where you can view its description, see which friends are using it, post comments on the Wall, and more.

NOTE: You can also find your way to the Apps Settings page through Facebook's Privacy features. When you open the privacy settings to the Apps options, you can click the **Edit Settings** button to visit the Apps Settings page.

Controlling App Privacy

One of the biggest behind-the-scenes aspects of any app is its sharing of your info. This is particularly true when your friends add new apps and allow them access to your info. As you can see from the Request for Permission pages you jump through to add an app (refer to Figure 13.5), shared information includes your basic profile info and email address, and can even include access to your photos and videos. Shared info also includes info about people on your friends list. Re-sharing is a default setting for just about everything on Facebook. The main reason behind all the openness of info sharing is it helps make the whole social network adventure more personalized, and more, well, *social*. Thankfully, through the Facebook Privacy settings, you can control what bits of information from your profile are utilized by the apps other people use.

To find your way to the privacy settings, click the drop-down arrow next to the **Home** button on any Facebook page and click **Privacy Settings**. This opens the Privacy Settings page. Click the **Edit Settings** button next to the **Apps and Websites** heading. This opens a page for controlling how apps, games, and websites use your data. Click the **Edit Settings** button next to the heading **How People Bring Your Info to Apps They Use**. This opens a dialog box by the same name, as shown in Figure 13.9. Here you can select which bits of information from your profile are shared with apps your friends use. After you've made your selections, click the **Save Changes** button.

FIGURE 13.9   You can specify exactly which bits of information are shared with apps by using this dialog box.

If you want to block all apps from any of your info, you must turn off all the platform's apps and websites.

Removing Apps

You can remove an application you no longer want or are no longer using. You might also remove applications to clean up your list just as a maintenance task. To delete an app, first open the Apps Settings page as described in the previous section. Next, click the **Delete** link (the X button to the far right of the application name). A prompt box appears. Click the **Remove** button to delete the application. Optionally, and depending on the application, you can rate the application or state a reason as to why you're removing it.

One more prompt box appears to let you know the application is gone. Click **Okay** to finish the process.

Summary

In this lesson, you learned how to use applications on Facebook. You learned how to find applications and add applications to your Facebook account. You also learned how to manage your apps. In the next lesson, you'll learn how to create Facebook Pages (with a capital *P*).

LESSON 14

Understanding Pages

In this lesson, you learn how to promote a business, brand, or public figure using Facebook Pages. You'll learn the differences between regular profile pages, groups, and specialty Pages. You'll also learn how to subscribe to Pages, create your own Page, and manage it as its administrator.

Page Basics

If you represent a company, organization, or professional group of some kind, you can create a presence on Facebook. Unlike individual profile pages, however, you need to create a special page—one that starts with a capital *P*. Facebook Pages are designed specifically for professional use and are completely separate from profile pages. A Page is a great way for fans to find you or your brand and spread the word about upcoming events, news, and information. Pages are a tool for connecting directly with customers or an audience, and even attracting future fans or buyers. Facebook members can choose to be fans or supporters of Pages.

Pages are an ideal public relations/marketing tool for the following:

- ▶ Public figures, such as politicians and government officials
- ▶ Celebrities
- ▶ Bands and musicians
- ▶ Artists
- ▶ Nonprofit organizations and charities
- ▶ Government agencies
- ▶ Large and small businesses
- ▶ Entertainment industries, such as television and radio
- ▶ Educational entities, such as schools, colleges, and universities
- ▶ Brand names and products, and the companies behind them

By using Pages, businesses, artists, and brands can interact with fans directly, going beyond one-directional conversation to dynamic communication. The content you post on a Page shows up in the news feeds of any fans or supporters, which in turn can be viewed by their friends, potentially driving up traffic to your Page and more customers to your door. As a marketing tool, Facebook Pages can help you increase product or brand awareness and interest, plus allow you more ways to communicate your message and receive feedback.

Pages, Profiles, or Groups?

Facebook users are often confused about the difference between profiles, groups, and Pages. Certainly a lot of similarities exist among the three; for example, Facebook features, such as the Wall, are readily available in each. Take a look at the Page for a television show shown in Figure 14.1.

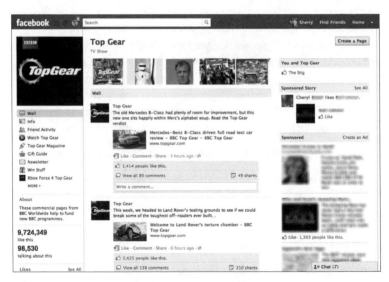

FIGURE 14.1   A Page for a popular cable television show.

At first glance, the Page looks similar to a regular profile or group page. It has a Wall for posting comments, a profile picture, a photo strip, and all the other regular Facebook features. Although it looks like a profile page, it's actually much more. To help you distinguish between Pages, profiles, and groups, however, take a look at some of the differences:

▶ Any individual can create a profile page, but only an authorized representative can create a professional Page. If you're not an authorized representative, you can create a group for the person or entity instead and invite other fans to participate. See Lesson 11, "Joining Groups," to learn more.

▶ Pages are also different in that you don't see who is actually administering the content. No one's name, other than the company or public figure, appears on the Pages.

▶ With a Page, you don't have to okay friend requests. Anyone who wants to be a fan is automatically approved when they click the **Like** button. This saves an administrator valuable time.

▶ Pages cannot invite people to be friends; rather, you can "like" a Page.

▶ Pages can integrate applications, contrasting with groups, which cannot add apps. With Pages, you can add apps such as Flash Player for uploading Flash files, YouTube Box to import your YouTube videos, or Simply RSS to import feeds.

▶ Unlike a regular profile page, a Page offers special administrator tools for collecting traffic and demographic information.

▶ A Page administrator can send out updates, such as a status posting or a link, to every fan or supporter.

▶ If you like a Page, the Page's administrator does not have access to your profile information.

▶ When you create a Page, it's indexed and searchable both inside and outside of Facebook.

▶ Tools for creating profiles and groups are readily available; however, tools for creating professional Pages are more difficult to locate on the site.

Basically, a Page is for promoting an entity or public figure, whereas a profile is just for individuals. Groups are informal fan-created pages, whereas Pages are authorized by the artist or company.

Strategies for Marketing with Pages

From a marketing standpoint, creating a Facebook Page for a business or public figure can really generate ongoing buzz about a product or promotion. One of the unique things about Pages is that you, as the administrator, can determine what tab on the Page users land on when they display your Page. You can use this strategy to direct a user to a specific ad campaign or action found on a custom tab on your Page. Take a look at Figure 14.2, for an example. It's a Page for a famous fast food chain. Notice you land on customized promotional artwork as soon as you display the Page.

FIGURE 14.2   A Page for a popular fast food chain with customized promotional artwork displayed.

As in the customized promotional art shown here, you can integrate all kinds of applications to engage the people who visit your Page. Hundreds of business-related apps are available to help you create all kinds of interesting and interactive content. For example, you can create quizzes, surveys, and games that keep users coming back for more. You can hold drawings and contests to bring back people frequently to the Page. Be sure to keep your Page content up-to-date and relevant. Utilize Facebook events to reach out to your fan base and let them know about upcoming calendar dates, engagements, concerts, rallies, or appearances.

As far as communication goes, responding promptly to fans who write on the Wall is also a good strategy, if applicable. If someone comments on a photo or video, keep the dialogue going. Fans and supporters want to hear back from you, and this medium is designed just for this type of activity. Failing to engage your fans and supporters results in lost opportunities to generate revenue and interest. Remember, Facebook is a social network first and foremost, designed to foster human interaction. Your marketing strategy should focus on this, too, to help extend your brand or message.

> NOTE: You can find numerous resources on the Internet to help you tap into the marketing and programming sides of Facebook, creating specialized apps and integrating others to suit your marketing needs. Sites like All Facebook (www.allfacebook.com) and Mashable (http://mashable.com) can offer some insights to get you started. Also be sure to check out Facebook's Developers page by clicking the **Developers** link at the bottom of any Facebook page.

Finding and Following Pages

From a fan or supporter standpoint, you can subscribe to a Page and get regular updates whenever new information is published. News appears as a story on the news feed on your Home page. Actually finding Pages to become a fan of takes a little effort on your part. One way to find a Page you like is to stumble across a story about one on your friends' profile pages or the stories that appear in the news feed or ticker on the Home page. Check your friends' Likes category on their profile page and see what Pages they're subscribing to or what public figures they're supporting. You can click the **Likes** category just below the cover photo to view all the Pages you're following.

You can also conduct a search for a particular name or product and see what's available on Facebook. Click in the **Search** box at the top of any Facebook page and type in the keyword or words you're searching for, such as a company or product name. Facebook immediately lists any potential matches; click the **See More Results** link at the bottom of the menu list to open the search results page, as shown in Figure 14.3. Click the **Pages** category to filter the view to any matching Pages.

FIGURE 14.3   The results page displays any matches.

When you find a Page you like, you can become a fan or supporter in just one click. Look for a **Like** button at the top of the Page. When you click the button, the page is added to your list of Likes.

After you're a fan, you're a subscribed member, so to speak. You'll now see stories from the Page out in the news feed. To find all the Pages you like in one spot, click the **Likes** link on your profile page (find it below the cover photo) to open the Favorites page, as shown in Figure 14.4. You can also find recently viewed pages listed under the Pages heading on your Home page (left column).

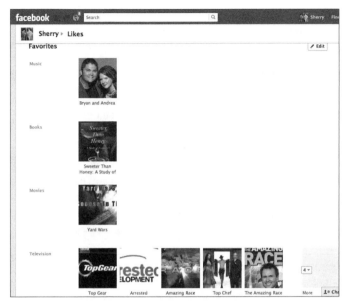

FIGURE 14.4   You can view your collection of Pages you like on the Favorites page accessed through your profile.

TIP: To unsubscribe from a Page, open the Page and look for an **Unlike** link or something similar. You'll find it on the far-left side as you scroll down the Page. Just click the link, and you're no longer a fan.

Creating and Managing a Page

If you're the official representative of a business, organization, or public figure, you can set up a Page in Facebook. Before you get started, take time to gather all the elements you need and save yourself some effort. Here are a few things you'll need:

▶ A name for the Page. The name you choose cannot be changed later—it's permanent (unless the Page is deleted entirely).

▶ A photo to act as the Page's profile picture.

▶ Information about the company, organization, or public figure. Information may include contact information, address, background story, company history, and so on.

▶ Content, such as pictures for a photo gallery or video clips, or content generated by apps.

▶ Choose a category, such as a local business, brand or product, or public figure. Facebook offers six main categories. Within each of these main categories are subcategories for defining exactly what kind of organization you represent, such as a grocery store or travel agency, actor or comedian, and so on. The category you choose has everything to do with how the Page is indexed on Facebook. It might help to research other Pages to see how they are categorized before attempting to create your own Page.

> CAUTION: If you're not authorized to create a Page and Facebook finds out, your account may be closed and the Page pulled from the site. Fan pages are not allowed unless created by an authorized person. If you would rather create a fan page, you can do so with a group. See Lesson 11 to learn more about groups.

Setting Up a New Page

After you've planned out what you need to display on the Page, you're ready to start building it. Follow these steps to create a new Page in Facebook:

1. If you're already logged on to your Facebook account, click the **Create a Page** link at the very bottom of the Home page.

2. Select the main category of Page you want to create. Each box displays a set of information you'll need to fill out. In Figure 14.5, for example, Brand or Product is selected and displayed.

3. Click the **Category** drop-down menu and choose a specific subcategory. Try to choose a category that best matches the type of Page you're creating.

4. Type in the name for the business, organization, product, or public figure.

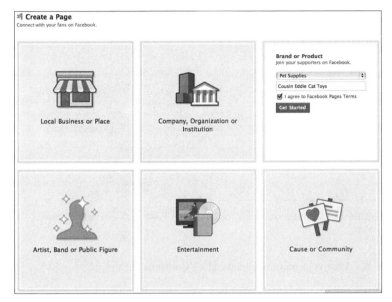

FIGURE 14.5 Start by choosing a type for your Page and entering the basic information.

NOTE: You cannot change the category later, so choose wisely. Facebook's form for Page creation has different fields for you to fill in based on which type of organization you select.

5. Click the terms of service check box.

6. Click the **Get Started** button.

NOTE: If you have not yet set up a Facebook account, you'll need to do so in order to create a Page. You can click the **Create a Page** link on the Facebook startup page and follow the prompts to create an account and a Page.

7. Next, Facebook steps you through three form pages for establishing your Page, not unlike the pages you saw when first creating your account. First, upload a picture to represent your Page, as prompted in Figure 14.6. The process for uploading a Page profile picture is the same as adding a regular profile picture.

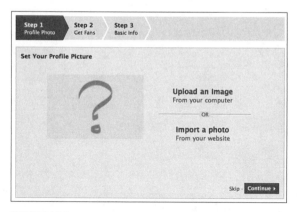

FIGURE 14.6   The next phase for creating a Page is to upload a profile picture.

8. After your picture uploads, click **Continue.**

9. The next phase is to find fans, as shown in Figure 14.7. You can invite people you already know on Facebook to like your Page, import contacts from another list, share a story about your new Page on your Wall, and automatically Like your Page.

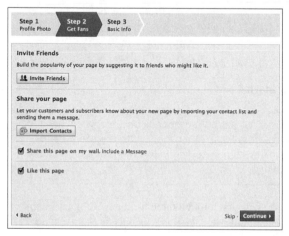

FIGURE 14.7   The next part of creating a Page is finding fans.

10. Make your selections, as needed, and click **Continue**.

11. Add information about your official website and write up a description about your Page in 255 words or less, as prompted in the screen shown in Figure 14.8.

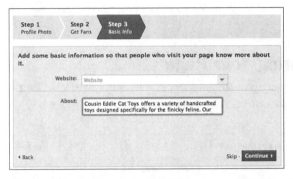

FIGURE 14.8 Type a brief description about your Page in this final form.

12. Click **Continue**. Facebook displays your new official Page, similar to that shown in Figure 14.9.

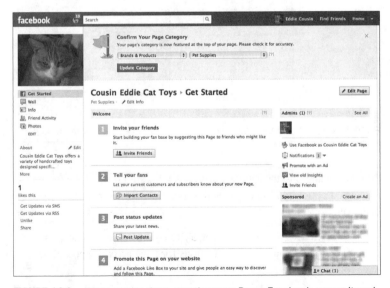

FIGURE 14.9 When you're done creating your Page, Facebook opens it and offers some help for fine-tuning the information.

After you've created your Page, follow the steps listed on the Welcome page to help you get started with fine-tuning your Page. Start by confirming your category and subcategory, as prompted at the top of the Page shown in Figure 14.9. You can also click the **Edit Page** button to specify options and settings for how your Page works (learn more about this in the next section). Use the links on the left to access various Page elements and features.

Administering Your Page

Managing a Page using your administrator powers is easy. Click the **Edit Page** link to open the settings shown in Figure 14.10.

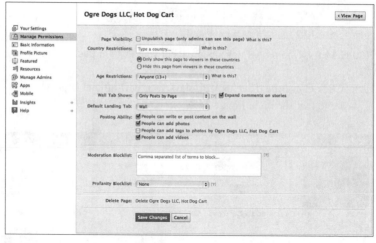

FIGURE 14.10   Open the Edit Page settings to make changes to various aspects of the Page.

To make changes to the settings, just click a link in the left pane to view associated options and settings. Here's a rundown of the editing categories displayed:

▶ **Your Settings**—Use this category to control your own posting preferences and email notifications for Page activities posted by others.

▶ **Manage Permissions**—Use this category to restrict the Page to a certain country or age group, as well as manage what sort of postings are allowed. You can also manage blocked users in this category, in case you need to control unfriendly posters.

▶ **Basic Information**—Click here to find settings for Page category, official Page name, contact information, description, and other basic info pertaining to the original category you assigned when creating the Page.

▶ **Profile Picture**—You can change your profile picture using these settings.

▶ **Featured**—When you like other professional Pages, Facebook lists them on your Page as featured likes, allowing users to click and visit the other Pages as well. The settings in this category let you control how this info is displayed on your Page.

▶ **Resources**—You'll find a plethora of resource links in this category to help you develop and market your Page.

▶ **Manage Admins**—If you need help managing your Page, you can add administrators using this category's settings.

▶ **Apps**—A listing of all the apps added to this Page appear here, including the default Facebook apps such as Photos.

▶ **Mobile**—You can set up your mobile device to update your Page using the settings in this category.

▶ **Insights**—Use Facebook's Insights tools to help you interpret and view data about the visitors and subscribers to your Page.

▶ **Help**—Click this link to go directly to the Help Center and view info about how to use Pages.

After your Page has been up and running for 48 hours, you can use the Insights feature to view data about demographics and activity of people accessing your Page.

To return to the Page after making changes, just click the **View Page** button at the top.

Advertising Your Page

You can use your advertising dollars to promote your Page on Facebook. Facebook offers two kinds of advertising: pay by clicks or pay by views (also called per-impression ads). With pay by clicks, you pay a set amount every time a user clicks your ad. With pay by views, you establish a price for 1,000 views of your ad. When creating an ad for Facebook, you can specify a target audience to help your ad reach the people you want. You can also specify a maximum amount to spend on the ad. You can learn all about advertising on Facebook by clicking the **Advertising** link at the bottom of any Facebook page. The Facebook Advertising page, shown in Figure 14.11, offers a step-by-step guide for planning and implementing an ad. You'll also find help with advertising regulations and rules on the site.

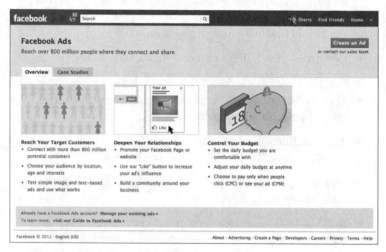

FIGURE 14.11   Facebook's Advertising feature offers step-by-step help with placing a promotional ad on the site.

If you already know exactly what kind of ad you want to create, click the **Promote with an Ad** link found on your Page. When clicked, the first form page opens to help you start designing and implementing your ad right away.

Summary

In this lesson, you learned how to use Pages on Facebook. You learned how to find and subscribe to Pages. You also saw how to make a new Page for your company or organization and then manage the Page after it's published. In the next lesson, you'll learn how to buy and sell stuff at the Facebook Marketplace.

The Facebook Marketplace

In this lesson, you learn how to sell stuff locally on Facebook. You'll also learn how to use the Marketplace app to browse items for sale and create your own listing.

What Is the Marketplace?

The Facebook Marketplace is a mutual effort from Facebook and Oodle, a network for classified ads online. Hoping to capture the growing Facebook user base, Facebook's Marketplace combines the social and interactive elements of its site with the growing popularity of online classifieds. Marketplace is another of Facebook's default applications available to all users. You can sell stuff in the Marketplace or buy stuff others are selling. You can search for specific items, sell items for a charity, or just see what everyone else is buying and selling online. You can sell household items, vehicles, and even houses in the Marketplace. You can also advertise for roommates, search for jobs, or look for an apartment to rent. The service is free, and best of all, you can conceivably know who you're buying from or selling to by checking out their profile pages when applicable. Listings are active for 30 days. Although the Marketplace app is integrated into Facebook, it's managed by Oodle. The Marketplace feature has been available for awhile now, but it's starting to pick up steam, particularly after the success of craigslist and the advent of another wave of new site upgrades to Facebook in the fall and winter of 2011/2012.

As with other online classified ad sites, in the Facebook Marketplace you can create listings for items you want to sell. Your listings can include a photo of the item, details about it, and why you're selling it. Other Facebook users can come along and view your listing, ask questions, add comments, and make a deal. Because of Facebook's viral nature, someone can come along and comment about a listing, such as "I have one of these and I love it," or "I want to give away my couch to charity, too," and spread the word quickly throughout their networks of friends. The sale or donation of an item can generate other interests, conversations, and so on. You may be surprised at the outcome, such as finding out that someone shares the same hobby or cause as you.

The Marketplace offers several categories for listings, including the following:

- ▶ **Merchandise**—This category is for items you want to sell, such as household items, furniture, baby clothes, books, and so on.

- ▶ **Cars**—This category is for listing cars, motorcycles, campers, vehicle parts, boats, and other motorized vehicles.

- ▶ **Rentals**—Use this category to find apartments to rent, room-mates, and short-term housing situations.

- ▶ **Real Estate**—Use this category to look for houses and condos for sale.

- ▶ **Jobs**—Use this category to look for full and part-time job opportunities.

- ▶ **Pets**—Looking for a new pet? Check out this category to find your next cat, dog, or hamster.

- ▶ **Tickets**—Find tickets to the hottest show or concert.

- ▶ **More**—This category opens more categories, such as links to community and service listings.

You peruse each category to see what's out there for sale. Each category features subcategories.

> CAUTION: Anytime you enter into the realm of buying and selling on the Internet, fraud and scam artists lurk around, ready to thwart your efforts. Be cautious, especially about deals that are too good to be true. Scammers offer all kinds of transactions that ultimately are illegal or rob you of your money, such as bounced checks, scams to send money to another country, or scams to steal your personal information. If your gut tells you something's wrong, it probably is. You can always report your suspicions; look for a Report This Listing link at the bottom of any ad. You can also alert Facebook when you encounter spam ads.

Navigating the Marketplace

To help you get a better idea of what you can do with the Marketplace, take a few moments to look around the pages. Figure 15.1 shows the Marketplace Home page, the "doorway," so to speak, to the online classified ads. You can access this page by clicking the **Marketplace** link on the Home page. The app's portal page displays featured sale items. You can start by browsing among the popular items, or jump right into browsing by category.

> NOTE: If you're a new Facebook user, you might not see the Marketplace app listed among your applications. If this is the case, you can conduct a search for it and authorize its use. Just type the keyword **Marketplace** in the Search box on the navigation bar, and then click the Marketplace App from the menu that appears. After you add the application, it will be available as a link on the Home page under the Apps category.

Figure 15.1 shows how easily you can browse around in the main categories and subcategories in the Marketplace. Across the top of the Marketplace Home page are tools for searching for listings and posting your own listings. For example, you can click the **Browse** button and choose a category to look through, or simply click a link in the left pane of the page.

Most important, you'll notice a location link. When clicked, it opens a Set Your Location box. You can click this box and specify an area where you want to shop. To set your Marketplace location, follow these steps:

1. Click in the **Location** link to display the Set Your Location dialog box shown in Figure 15.2.

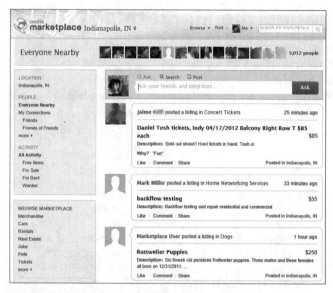

FIGURE 15.1   Facebook's Marketplace gateway.

FIGURE 15.2   You can specify a Marketplace location.

2. Click the **Country** box and type in or select a country.

3. Click the **Location** box and type in a city and state, preferably a city near you.

4. Click the **Make this my Home Location** check box to make this your default location setting.

5. Click **Set Location**.

Facebook changes the Marketplace page to reflect the new location setting. You can now peruse listings in your area.

Browsing the Listings

You can search for a specific item in the Marketplace, or browse the listings to see what people are selling in your area. For example, to look for items being offered for sale, look among the Merchandise category. To browse, just click a subcategory under any main category area. Facebook opens a results page, similar to Figure 15.3.

As you peruse the listings, you can click a listing title to open its page. The listing page opens, as shown in Figure 15.4. It includes the seller's profile picture, details about the item for sale, a place for a photo of the item, recent or similar listings, and an area to ask a question or leave a comment. If you're interested in the item, click the **I'm Interested** button and send the seller a message. You can also use the listing's Comments area to ask a question.

FIGURE 15.3 You can leisurely browse through the various subcategories to see what items are listed in your area.

FIGURE 15.4   A typical ad listing on the Marketplace.

You can click the **Share** button to open the Share dialog box and post a link to the ad on your profile page, or send a link to a friend to check out.

To search for a specific item, click in the Search box at the top of any Marketplace page and type in the keyword or words you want to look up. Press **Enter** or **Return**, and Facebook displays any matching results. Facebook keeps track of your typed searches and lists them on the results page in case you want to use them again at a later time; just click the text to conduct a search.

In previous versions of the Marketplace app, you could easily return to Facebook using a button at the top of the screen. As of this writing, such a link doesn't exist. They might change this as they continue to work on the app, but for now, you'll need to type in the www.facebook.com address in your browser to get back to your Facebook account.

Adding Your Own Listing

You can easily create your own ads in the Marketplace. To start a listing, click the **Post** button at the top of the Marketplace page. This opens the Post a Listing box, as shown in Figure 15.5. You may be prompted to allow Marketplace access to your profile first, but just okay the procedure and continue.

Begin filling out the required fields in the form. As soon as you choose a category, the box expands to reveal more form fields, as shown in Figure 15.6.

FIGURE 15.5   Use the Post a Listing box to start your ad.

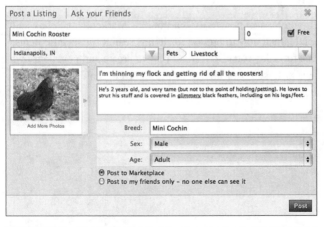

FIGURE 15.6   The Post a Listing form expands as you fill it out to reveal more details you can add.

Fill in the rest of the information as applicable. Explain why you're selling the item and add any detailed information about it. You can use the Photo field to upload a photo of the item. You can also choose to post the item to friends only or to everyone on Facebook. When you've finished filling out the details, click the **Post** button. Facebook then asks whether you want to publish the ad on your news feed.

Finally, if this is your first time selling an item, the Marketplace app displays a Request for Permission page; click **Allow**.

After you post an ad, monitoring it, answering any questions that arise, and figuring out how a buyer pays you when you reach an agreed-upon price are all up to you. Because the Marketplace is designed to be local in nature, you can expect buyers to pick up the item at an arranged time and place, and pay with cash. Facebook's Marketplace does not offer a money service, such as eBay's PayPal, so you're really left to your own devices.

To view your listings, click the **My Account** link. This opens a page where you can view active listings, expired listings, responses, and so on.

To end a listing, after it's sold or when you give up on selling it, you can revisit the My Account page, open the listing page, and click the **Close** link.

Summary

In this lesson, you learned how to use Facebook's Marketplace to buy and sell items. You learned how to browse for items, search for specific items, and view items for sale. You also learned how to create and post your own listing. In the next lesson, you'll learn how to take Facebook on the road with you using the mobile features.

LESSON 16

Making Facebook Mobile

In this lesson, you learn how Facebook's mobile features work. You'll learn how to activate the texting feature to send and receive Facebook information and how to browse Facebook's mobile website using the special URL. Plus, you'll find out how easy it is to upload photos or videos from your cell phone's camera.

Overview of Facebook's Mobile Features

If you simply cannot get enough of Facebook on your computer, you'll be happy to know you can access it through your mobile device and have Facebook at your fingertips wherever you go. You can use the Facebook Mobile app to send text updates and messages from your phone to your profile page, receive notifications about friend requests, status updates, and other posts from your friends. Facebook also offers apps for smart phones and the iPad (see Figure 16.1) for a fuller social networking experience.

To use apps for the iPad or a smart phone (such as the Android), visit Facebook's Help Center. Click the navigation bar's drop-down arrow and select **Account Settings**. Click the **Mobile** tab, and then click the **Facebook Mobile** link.

If you don't have a smart phone or an iPad, you can still access Facebook from your phone. In fact, you can use Facebook's mobile features to send and receive status updates, messages, photos, and more. You can tell Facebook to send you specific users' status updates, as well as let you know in what time frame the updates occurred. Sounds fun, right?

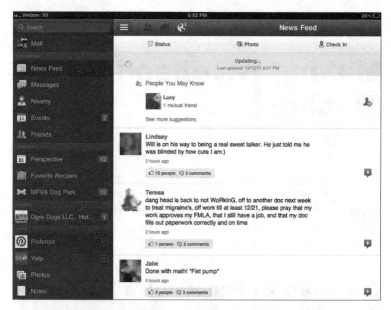

FIGURE 16.1   The Facebook for iPad app lets iPad users access the Facebook interface in a slightly abbreviated format.

Text messaging is pretty standard mobile technology these days, and if your mobile device supports such features, chances are good that you can use it with Facebook's mobile capabilities. All text messages use a standardized mobile text transfer method, called SMS, which stands for *Short Message Service*, or MMS, short for *Multimedia Messaging Service*. If your mobile device supports SMS, you can send and receive text messages from Facebook. Depending on your service, you might be limited as to the number and size of the messages (up to 140 characters). If your device supports MMS, you can go a step further and upload photos from your cell phone, for example, and post them onto your Facebook profile page.

If your mobile device features web browsing capabilities, you can visit Facebook directly—in miniature form, of course—using the http://m.facebook.com URL. You can do just about everything on the small-scale page as you can on your full-blown web browser page. You can view and change your status, check your friends' statuses, track events, view the news feed stories, view photos, and see what's happening in your favorite Facebook groups. You cannot visit Facebook's website without web browsing capabilities, however, even if your cell phone has text messaging features.

Activating Facebook Mobile for Text Messages

You can use your cell phone's text messaging features to send and receive text to your Facebook account. For example, you can update your status, post a comment on someone's profile, or send someone a message. Before you can start taking Facebook on the road with you, though, you first have to activate the feature to work with your mobile device. Follow these steps:

1. Click the drop-down arrow button next to the Home button on the navigation bar and select **Account Settings**.

2. Click the **Mobile** link to display the Mobile Settings, as shown in Figure 16.2.

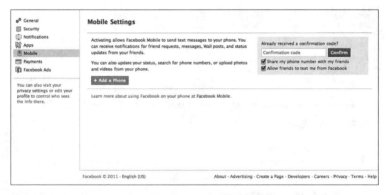

FIGURE 16.2   You can set up mobile texting through Account Settings.

3. Click **Add a Phone**. Facebook might require you to type in your password again to proceed.

The Confirm a Phone Number dialog box appears, as shown in Figure 16.3.

FIGURE 16.3   The Confirm a Phone Number box.

4. Use the drop-down menu to select your country code.

5. Type in your mobile phone number.

6. Select whether you want to send a confirmation via text or voice call.

7. Click **Continue**. Another prompt box appears, as shown in Figure 16.4, asking for a confirmation code.

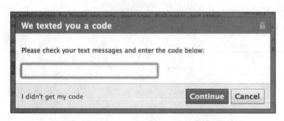

FIGURE 16.4   Enter your confirmation code here.

8. When you receive the confirmation code from Facebook (check your mobile device; the process could take several minutes), type the code in the field shown.

If you do not receive a confirmation code in a reasonable amount of time, click the **I Didn't Get My Code** link.

9. Click **Continue**. A prompt box appears declaring the procedure a success, as shown in Figure 16.5, with further options you can designate.

FIGURE 16.5   Before you exit, choose to activate text messages.

10. Click **Submit**.

Facebook adds the mobile device information to the Mobile tab of your
Account Settings page (see Figure 16.6), and you can start sending and
receiving text messages with Facebook.

FIGURE 16.6   You can edit your mobile settings as needed.

NOTE: If you run in to any trouble using Facebook's mobile features, be sure to consult the Help Center to find answers. Click the
Account menu (the drop-down arrow on the Navigation bar) and
click **Help**.

Anytime you want to edit the settings, open Account Settings to the Mobile tab and click an **Edit** link, and you can adjust the settings as needed.

> TIP: If you switch cell phone carriers later, you can revisit the Mobile tab on your Account Settings page and remove the old phone and add the new one using these same steps.

Sending Text Messages from a Mobile Device

Now that you've activated your mobile account, you can start sending and receiving Facebook data. How does that work exactly? You can send messages using the codes listed in Table 16.1. The codes and text you send are directed to the 32665 number, which happens to spell FBOOK if you prefer keyboard letters rather than numbers. When directing your text to a specific Facebook user, be sure to use the person's full name. If there are other members with the same name, Facebook will ask you to confirm from a list of candidates it messages back to you. Simply make the correct choice, and on goes the message to the proper recipient.

TABLE 16.1   Facebook Texting Codes

Action	Code	Sample
Update your status	(no code needed)	is visiting a museum!
Write on someone's wall	wall	wall bob smith congrats on the promotion.
Send a message msg	msg	msg gail jones Hi, how r u?
Search for profile info	srch or search	srch bob smith or search bob smith
Get a cell number	cell	cell bob smith
Poke someone	poke	poke gail jones
Send a friend request	add	add bill miller
Write a note	note	note I'm having a great time in Florida
Find help with texting	help	help

> TIP: If your cell phone or mobile device features web browsing capabilities, you can access the mobile Facebook website: http://m.facebook.com. Use your mobile device's web browser to navigate to the URL, and then log in using your account name and password.

Uploading Photos or Videos

You can upload photos or videos you take with your cell phone and add them to your Facebook profile page. You can do this only if your cell phone supports MMS protocols. All you have to do is upload the photo or video to mobile@facebook.com.

If the phone you're using hasn't already been confirmed with Facebook's site, they'll send you a confirmation code the first time you try an upload task. You'll have to log in to Facebook and enter the code on the Account Settings page in the Mobile tab (refer to Figure 16.6). After you've confirmed the phone, you can use it to upload more photos or videos to your profile page.

To learn more about uploading and editing photos, see Lesson 9, "Sharing Photos." To learn how to upload videos, see Lesson 10, "Sharing Videos."

> TIP: Your mobile page may list a personalized upload email address you can use to post status updates or upload photos to your profile. The email address is assigned randomly by Facebook. Just look for the link to utilize the feature.

Summary

In this lesson, you learned how to use Facebook's mobile features. You learned how to activate your Facebook Mobile account and send status updates from your cell phone. You also learned how to text messages and other Facebook actions to your friends. You found out how to access Facebook using a web browser on a mobile device, and how to upload photos and videos to your profile page.

Now that you've completed the final lesson, you're ready to venture out on your own and explore Facebook with confidence. Good luck and happy networking—socially speaking, that is. I'll see you online!

Index

A

abuse, reporting, 90

access, controlling account access, 80-81

accessing account info, 26

account access, controlling, 80-81

account info, accessing, 26

account security, 31

Account Settings page, 26

accounts, signing up for, 13-18

activating Facebook Mobile for text messages, 199-201

Activity Log, 45
    viewing, 45-46

adding
    cover photos, 42-43
    listings to Marketplace, 195-196
    photos, 110
        photo albums, 111-113
    profile info, 20-22
    profile pictures, 17, 22-23
    videos, 124-127

administering Pages, 184-185

ads, 57

advertising, Pages, 186

albums
    deleting, 119
    editing, 117-121

app requests, responding to, 165-168

application settings, changing, 169-171

apps, 161-162
    blocking, 88-89
    browsing with Apps Dashboard, 168-169
    controlling, 85-87
    controlling privacy, 171-172
    finding, 164
    for iPad, 197
    kinds of, 162-163
    managing, 169
    privacy, 162
    removing, 172
    responding to app requests, 165-168
    searching for with keywords, 169

Apps Dashboard, browsing apps, 168-169

avatars, 22. *See also* profile pictures

B

Birthday Cards, 163
birthdays, 57
blocking people and apps, 88-89
blogging with Notes, 98-100
breached accounts, 80
browsing
    apps with Apps Dashboard, 168-169
    Marketplace, 193-194

C

categories, Marketplace, 190
changing
    application settings, 169-171
    profile pictures, 43-45
    status, 24-26
Chat bar, 102
chatting with friends, 101-103
closed groups, 137
communicating through Facebook, 91-92
    blogging with Notes, 98-100
    chatting with friends, 101-103
    managing messages, 94-95
    sending and receiving messages, 92-94
    sending messages, 95-96
    sharing links, 96-98
content, 31
    sharing, 30
controlling
    account access, 80-81
    app privacy, 171-172
    apps and websites, 85-87
    how you connect, 82-84
    tags, 84-85

cover photos, adding, 42-43
creating events, 156-159
customizing privacy settings, 81-83

D

deleting
    albums, 119
    groups, 148

E

Edit Album page, 117
editing
    albums, 117-121
    friends, 68
    photos, 116, 120
    videos, 129-130
etiquette, 32
    do's, 32-33
    don'ts, 33-34
events, 57
    creating, 156-159
    finding, 153-154
    managing, 159-160
    overview, 151-153
    private events, 152
    public events, 152
    responding to, 155-156
    searching for, 154-155

F

Facebook, 5-6
    features, 8-9
    history of, 7-8
Facebook Mobile, 197-198
    activating for text messages, 199-201

FarmVille, 163

features of Facebook, 8-9

feed stories, 51

finding

    apps, 164

    events, 153-154

    friends, 16, 63

        looking up friends, 63-66

        responding to friends who find you, 67

    groups, 138

    help with Help Center, 34-36

    pages, 177-179

Flixter, 163

following pages, 177-179

friends

    chatting with, 101-103

    editing, 68

    finding, 16, 63

        looking up friends, 63-66

        responding to friends who find you, 67

    mutual friends, 67

    organizing into lists, 70-73

    subscribing to people, 75-76

    tagging in photos, 120

    unfriending, 74-75

    viewing, 68, 70

G

groups, 135-137

    closed groups, 137

    deleting, 148

    finding, 138

    joining, 138-140

    managing, 145-148

    open groups, 137

    versus profiles and pages, 174-175

    removing members, 148

    secret groups, 137

    starting your own, 141-145

H

help, finding with Help Center, 34-36

Help Center, 34-36

Help Center page, 35

history of Facebook, 7-8

Home page, 9-10, 52

    left pane, 55-56

    navigation bar, 52-54

    right pane, 56-57

How Tags Work privacy category, 84

How You Connect settings, 82-84

Hughes, Chris, 7

I

Inside Facebook blog, 37

iPad, apps for, 197

iPhoto Exporter, 113

J

joining groups, 138-140

K

keywords, searching for apps, 169

L

left pane of Home page, 55-56
limiting past posts, 87-88
links, sharing, 96, 98
Links app, 98
listings
    adding to Marketplace,
        195-196
    browsing Marketplace, 193-194
lists, organizing friends into, 70-73
looking up friends, 63-66

M

Mafia Wars, 163
Manage Blocking page, 89
managing
    apps, 169
    events, 159-160
    groups, 145-148
    messages, 94-95
    Pages, 179-180
Marketing, strategies for marketing
    with Pages, 176
Marketplace, 189-190
    adding listings, 195-196
    browsing, 193-194
    categories, 190
    navigating, 191-193
    searching, 193
    setting location, 191
messages
    managing, 94-95
    sending, 95-96
    sending and receiving, 92-94
mini-feeds, 51

mobile devices
    sending text messages from,
        202-203
    uploading photos or videos, 203
Moskovitz, Dustin, 7
mutual friends, 67
MyCalendar, 163

N

navigating Marketplace, 191-193
navigation bar, 52-54
news feeds, 51, 58-60
Notes, blogging, 98-100
notifications, 52, 60-61

O

open groups, 137
organizing
    friends into lists, 70-73
    photos, 116, 120

P

pages, 19, 173-174
    administering, 184-185
    advertising, 186
    creating and managing, 179-180
    finding, 177-179
    following, 177-179
    setting up new, 180-184
    strategies for marketing, 176
    unsubscribing from, 179
    versus profiles and groups,
        174-175

people
    blocking, 88-89
    subscribing to, 75-76
photo albums, starting, 111-113
photos
    adding, 110
        photo albums, 111-113
    editing, 116, 120
    organizing, 116, 120
    sharing, 105-108
        iPhoto Exporter, 113
    tagging, 114-116
    tagging friends, 120
    uploading with mobile
        devices, 203
Photos page, viewing, 108-110
pictures
    cover photos, adding, 42-43
    profile pictures
        adding, 22-23
        changing, 43-45
player controls, videos, 128
Poke, 58
posting on friend's timeline, 49
posts
    limiting past posts, 87-88
    removing
        from the Wall, 148
        from timeline, 49-50
privacy, 30, 77-78
    apps, 162, 171-172
    protection strategies, 78-79
privacy settings
    blocking people and apps,
        88-89
    customizing, 81-83
    limiting past posts, 87-88

private events, 152
profile info, adding, 20-22
profile pages, 10
profile pictures
    adding, 17, 22-23
    changing, 43-45
profiles
    adding profile info, 20-22
    building, 19
    versus pages and groups,
        174-175
protection strategies, 78-79
public events, 152
Publisher, 48

R

receiving messages, 92-94
recording videos, 131-134
removing
    apps, 172
    members of groups, 148
    posts
        from the wall, 148
        from timeline, 49-50
reporting abuse, 90
responding
    to app requests, 165-168
    to events, 155-156
    to friends who find you, 67
right pane of Home page, 56-57

S

safety, 31
Saverin, Eduardo, 7

searching
　　for apps with keywords, 169
　　for events, 154-155
　　Marketplace, 193
secret groups, 137
security, 77-78
　　accounts, 31
　　protection strategies, 78-79
Security Check screen, 15
sending
　　messages, 92-96
　　text messages from mobile
　　　devices, 202-203
sharing
　　content and information, 30
　　links, 96, 98
　　photos, 105-108
　　　iPhoto Exporter, 113
　　videos, 123-124
Sign Up page, 14
signing up for accounts, 13-18
spammers, 137
sponsored ads, 57
starting groups, 141-145
status
　　changing, 24-26
　　updating on timeline, 47-49
stories, 47, 51
stream, 51
subscribing to people, 75-76
subscriptions, 75

T

tagging
　　friends in photos, 120
　　photos, 114-116

tags, controlling, 84-85
terms of service, 29-32
text messages
　　activating Facebook Mobile for,
　　　199-201
　　sending from mobile devices,
　　　202-203
ticker, 56
timeline, 19
　　basics of, 39-42
　　posting on a friend's timeline,
　　　49
　　removing posts, 49-50
　　status, updating, 47-49
　　stories, 47
tour of Facebook, 9-10

U

unfriending friends, 74-75
unsubscribing from pPages, 179
updating status timeline, 47-49
uploading
　　photos with mobile
　　　devices, 203
　　videos with mobile devices, 203

V

videos
　　adding, 124-127
　　editing, 129-130
　　recording, 131-134
　　sharing, 123-124
　　uploading with mobile
　　　devices, 203
　　viewing, 127-129

viewing
> Activity Log, 45-46
> friends, 68, 70
> Photos page, 108-110
> videos, 127-129

W

Wall, 39
We're Related, 162

websites, controlling, 85-87
Welcome page, 18

Y

YoVille, 163

Z

Zuckerberg, Mark, 7

Sams**TeachYourself**

from Sams Publishing

Sams **Teach Yourself in 10 Minutes**
offers straightforward, practical answers
for fast results.

These small books of 250 pages or less
offer tips that point out shortcuts and
solutions, cautions that help you avoid
common pitfalls, and notes that explain
additional concepts and provide additional
information. By working through the
10-minute lessons, you learn everything
you need to know quickly and easily!

When you only have time for the answers,
Sams Teach Yourself books are your
best solution.

Visit **informit.com/samsteachyourself**
for a complete listing of the products
available.

Sams Teach Yourself
Facebook
in 10 Minutes

FREE
Online Edition

Safari
Books Online

Your purchase of *Sams Teach Yourself Facebook in 10 Minutes* includes access to a free online edition for 45 days through the **Safari Books Online** subscription service. Nearly every Sams book is available online through **Safari Books Online**, along with thousands of books and videos from publishers such as Addison-Wesley Professional, Cisco Press, Exam Cram, IBM Press, O'Reilly Media, Prentice Hall, Que, and VMware Press.

Safari Books Online is a digital library providing searchable, on-demand access to thousands of technology, digital media, and professional development books and videos from leading publishers. With one monthly or yearly subscription price, you get unlimited access to learning tools and information on topics including mobile app and software development, tips and tricks on using your favorite gadgets, networking, project management, graphic design, and much more.

Activate your FREE Online Edition at
informit.com/safarifree

STEP 1: Enter the coupon code: JSIVHFH.

STEP 2: New Safari users, complete the brief registration form.
Safari subscribers, just log in.

If you have difficulty registering on Safari or accessing the online edition,
please e-mail customer-service@safaribooksonline.com